A PATCH
MADE IN
Heaven

A PATCH
MADE IN
Heaven

A PATCH
MADE IN
Heaven

*A year of birdwatching
in one place*

DOMINIC COUZENS

ROBERT HALE · LONDON

© Dominic Couzens 2012
First published in Great Britain 2012

ISBN 978-0-7090-9112-7

Robert Hale Limited
Clerkenwell House
Clerkenwell Green
London EC1R 0HT

www.halebooks.com

The right of Dominic Couzens to be identified as
author of this work has been asserted by him
in accordance with the Copyright, Designs and
Patents Act 1988

Illustrations by Dave Nurney

A catalogue record for this book is available from the British Library

4 6 8 10 9 7 5 3

Typeset by e-type, Liverpool
Printed in Great Britain by MPG Books Group,
Bodmin and King's Lynn

CONTENTS

ACKNOWLEDGEMENTS

Books are always an ordeal for a writer's family, and this one, which included hundreds of trips to a draughty lake down the road, required a more than usual level of tolerance from my wonderful wife Carolyn, and children Emily and Samuel. My heartfelt thanks to them.

In writing the book I have been cajoled and encouraged greatly by Alexander Stilwell at Hale, to whom special thanks are due. Martin Diggle did a great editing job and I also thank Nikki Edwards for bringing the project to fruition. Carole Vincer did a terrific job of converting my scrawl into a map.

Big thanks to my friend and colleague Dave Nurney for his inspired, crisp line drawings that add so much to the book, and for the front cover. Nice work, mate.

Finally, thanks to the employees of Sembcorp, especially Peter Ferenczy, Roger Harrington, Ian Hayward and Jon Morley, who have allowed me to traipse all over the site that they manage, and have all been a great help throughout. Special thanks too to my co-patchworkers Trevor Thorpe and Chris Parnell, who have flogged the site with the same enthusiasm as I over the years. Thanks for the shared bird sightings – and here's to the mega-rarity that we are all hoping for.

FOREWORD

The Wildlife Trusts:
help protect your local patch

The protection of places for wildlife is a founding principle of The Wildlife Trusts.

It was Charles Rothschild, founder of the organization that we know today as The Wildlife Trusts, who scoured the UK countryside a hundred years ago, supported by some of the country's finest naturalists, looking for places worthy of protection.

Rothschild's vision of protecting places for wildlife has shaped the development of the nature conservation movement as we know it. The current network of protected sites includes 2,300 Wildlife Trust nature reserves – some of them still home to the rare butterflies, wildflowers, veteran trees and sparkling clear streams he and his colleagues surveyed and sought to protect. These places are now the building blocks for restoring nature more widely in urban areas and across the wider countryside. For many of us they are our local 'patch'. They are places we become familiar with – when we visit in the spring to catch a display of orchids – and where we can escape to and immerse ourselves in nature for a while.

As well as caring for wildlife on our own nature reserves, The Wildlife Trusts work with landowners and farmers to create, restore and maintain wildlife habitats. Our vision of A Living Landscape sees wildlife moving freely through the countryside, through towns and cities.

By creating bigger, interconnected networks of wildlife habitats to re-establish wildlife populations, we can help achieve nature's recovery. And a resilient and healthy environment provides ecological security for people too, safeguarding the natural services we all depend on, like clean air, clean water and carbon storage.

The Wildlife Trusts are passionate about wildlife and our work doesn't stop at the shoreline. The Wildlife Trusts also have a vision for Living Seas, where wildlife thrives from the depths of the ocean to the coastal shallows. All across the UK we are inspiring people about marine life and carrying out vital research to help protect basking sharks, dolphins, seals, corals and a host of rare and fragile marine habitats.

The Wildlife Trusts want people to be inspired about the future of their own local patch so they value it, understand their relationship with it and act to protect it.

To help make this happen, Wildlife Trusts all over the UK work within their local communities to effect real change. We work with businesses, schools, community groups and other environmental organizations to manage land for wildlife. With shrinking natural habitats in many towns and cities, gardens and gardeners have an ever increasing role to play in helping wildlife.

To find out how you can get involved in helping to protect your local patch go to www.wildlifetrusts.org/yourlocaltrust and follow the links to your local Wildlife Trust's website.

INTRODUCTION

Welcome to my Patch. Since – although it's not – I view it as 'mine', I dignify it with initial capitals, as though it were a small country, and often even give it the definite article – The Patch – as though it were the only one. This, of course, is by no means the case; many other people have their patches and I'm sure they will name and style them as they please.

This book covers a year in the wildlife of a small area in southern England, covering the comings and goings of wildlife there, particularly the birds, and how these change from month to month. It is a diary of an area no more than one square kilometre and is thus southern England in miniature, a tiny speck of the whole.

Welcome, at the same time, to the land of Any Patch. The idea of this book isn't for me to luxuriate in the delights of my own personal speck of land, but actually to reflect on what any division of land – yours or mine – might offer over the course of the wildlife year. In this way it isn't really a diary, more of a guidebook. After all, when swallows fly over my Patch in the spring and autumn, they do so everywhere, and do the same things, arouse the same emotions and have the same intentions that all swallows do. In the same way, about the same time that jays begin collecting acorns, foxes begin to scream and butterflies begin to emerge in my Patch, they will do so everywhere, including the piece of ground that you call yours. So I hope that this diary will resonate with your own wildlife experiences, too.

Before going further, let me explain more fully what I really mean by a 'patch'. Everybody knows that a patch is a fragment, and a patch of land is similarly a fragment of land. But in birding parlance a patch, more properly called a 'local patch', is the place where we do most of our birdwatching and can follow the ebb and flow of their seasonal movements. It is our birdwatching home. It is invariably close enough to where we actually live that we can pop in with great frequency to see what is about. Over the course of years the patch, as mentioned above, becomes 'yours'. You don't own it, but you are probably there more frequently than the owners themselves are. Over those same years you become familiar with the birds and animals that are there, so that you immediately notice when something has changed. You can compare one year with another, and watch animals' fortunes rise and fall. You cannot miss freakish events, such as the extraordinary invasion of painted lady butterflies described in the chapter on May, and the chances are that you will spot many things that casual visitors to your patch won't even notice.

It is possible that you might have thought such wildlife-watching rhythms didn't exist in today's world. In our sensation-hungry media, the usual birdwatchers depicted are the fanatics, the ones who travel around the country in search of rare birds to tick off their list, and in doing so tend to excite a degree of derision. In reality, very few people live up to this model, and there are many more thousands who actually do most of their birdwatching close to where they sleep at night. These people are 'patch-watchers'. And even the rarity hunters filmed by the media at their worst are usually dedicated patch-watchers on a day out.

What makes somebody settle upon their own patch, and how can you choose your own? First of all, as mentioned above, a patch needs to be local, preferably a few minutes by car or foot away from where the enthusiast lives. I know a keen birder who has a twenty-minute drive to his patch (admittedly it is Titchwell, one of the best single sites for birds in the whole of Britain), but in my opinion that is too far. It needs to be close by. But not too close, either. It shouldn't be your garden, unless you have lots of land with varied habitat.

Most patches are small. You might want to try to cover the whole of the Yorkshire Dales National Park, but that probably won't work. You cannot cover such an area effectively or ever feel that it is really 'yours'. It needs to be small enough for it to be a genuine choice. It also needs to be small enough that you can cover it in a few hours, otherwise you will be tearing this way and that, never settling and actually enjoying yourself, which is what patch-watching is about.

The other essential for a local patch is that it has some wildlife to interest you, and this is where your choice really becomes important. If you are a passionate birdwatcher you will really need an area with a decent mix of habitats, and preferably some water, so that, quite frankly, you won't get bored by seeing the same species again and again and again. But if you are mad about beetles, or moths, you will more easily be delighted by a single patch of woodland. Yet I find that, as far as birds are concerned, woods rarely fit the bill because it is hard to appreciate the birds' movements, and a wood's rhythms are closely similar year on year. It is also hard to see clear sky, the source of much of your year's variety.

Other than that, of course, there is no definition of a local patch. A patch is a state of mind rather than a place, a type of wildlife appreciation rather than a specific location. Yours and mine are different, but our overall experiences are broadly shared. So this book is actually a description of what might be happening in the bird community and among other wildlife almost anywhere in Britain.

It is also, I suppose, a year in the life of a birdwatcher. It would be wrong to assume that a local patch is anything but an artificial, human concept. After all, nobody sees everything on their patch in any given year, and much of what they do see is merely a snapshot in the day of whatever creatures they are seeing – a fragment of a patch, one might say. So this brings us back to the essence of the book, which is a wildlife diary.

Why, you might ask, write a wildlife diary for a local patch? The reason is simple: that I want to confirm to you that you can find some of Britain's most interesting wildlife on your doorstep. There is wonder and intrigue close at hand. For many years we have all been able to become goggle-eyed with wonder in front of our TV screens, as film-makers have brought us the world's wonders through a lens: flamingos in Africa, koalas in Australia and penguins in Antarctica, for example. In recent years there has been a welcome celebration of what can be found in Britain, from otters in Birmingham to blue tits in Norfolk (via an awful lot of deer – please, no more deer!). But watching wildlife on TV is not the same as finding it for yourself, and people throughout the land are still reluctant to believe that *they* can find amazing things for themselves. The essence of following a patch is exactly that: to find things yourself and uncover your own personal wonders.

Finally, though, are there deeper motives for writing a book about a single small piece of God's earth that is forever England? Yes, if you will forgive me and not blush, it is hopefully to impart some joy, and encourage you to find your own. The world is fast-moving, confusing and not very peaceful, but a small patch of it can be the opposite. The rhythms of nature are quite slow and unhurried; the return of migrants and changing of colours and seasons are reassuring, not confusing; and any patch, when it is home and when it is familiar, can engender peace and calm, even if it is busy with people. When the birds are not there and the weather is bad it can induce great irritation and frustration, too, of course. But these are the sorts of suffering that are trivial, and harmless, and will actually help us to enjoy the best times. Joy is a precious commodity, and it doesn't come in a rush or a fog of the mind.

So please read this book to enjoy it. But more importantly, find joy in your own patch, wherever that is.

MY PATCH

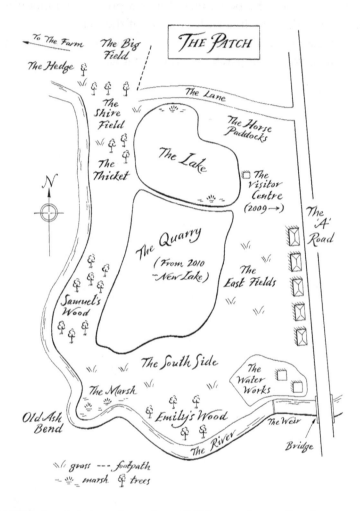

This book is based on the wildlife year in my Patch, so you had better come on a guided tour around the area. In conjunction with the map, you will get an overview of what

the place is like. In the map I have used imprecise and sometimes fictional names to describe the areas on The Patch, and
these are continued in the narrative of the diary. They are all
real locations, of course, but the reason for using general terms
is to allow them to relate to places that you might find on your
own patch (e.g. The Lake). As I said, this is a book about any
patch, not just mine.

Now, it would be easy enough to tour the site by means of a
detailed empirical description, mentioning geographical
features and vegetation and other such delights. But perhaps
that would bore readers stiff and hasten you, if not to another
part of the book, then possibly to another book entirely.
Instead, therefore, I will describe the area bit by bit as I personally discovered it, which was in a distinctly piecemeal manner
over quite a number of years. This is another feature of patch-
watching. It usually takes a long time to uncover all the parts of
your area, unless it is very small, and the process of finding out
which areas are best for certain things, such as summer
migrants / breeding birds / butterflies, etc. is usually protracted.
Furthermore, over the years patches change, often radically,
and this has certainly been the case with mine.

Anyway, let's get away on this tour. Walking in from the north,
a dirt track soon reaches the corner of a lake set in farmland
beside a river. The lake, which I will henceforth imaginatively
name The Lake, is actually a loaded gravel pit about 1.2 hectares
in extent, fringed with a few desultory patches of reeds here and
there, and one or two willows. None of the reed-beds is more
than a couple of metres thick, but they still hide reed warblers in
the summer and water rails in the winter. Yet the aspect of The
Lake is very open, and the reeds barely make an impact on the
place, and if reed stems could talk, I'm sure they would much
rather be part of a dense, wide bed that could make a satisfying
whisper, instead of a whimper, on a windy day.

These days one can climb a stile and walk all around The
Lake, but on that magic day on 21 March 2002 when my wife

and I first stumbled upon this place, it was protected by a barbed wire fence and we could only peer upon its bare, stony, unfilled bottom (it was filled with water later that year). Doubtless the high fence was there for our protection, but at the time it was easy to imagine a building hidden behind it that was a centre for the testing of chemical weapons. Later on, the gravel extraction company placed exciting yellow signs telling us of guard dog patrols. But if they were there I never saw them, and I don't know of anybody who did. They were as rare as the two-headed foxes and gulls that I could have sworn I saw there occasionally through the mist of dusk.

Although The Lake was unfilled and not yet unveiled, the farmland to the west proved to be an attraction from the start, with its singing skylarks and hovering kestrels. On the north-west corner of The Patch that farmland amounted to a huge cultivated field, usually planted with ley. The field, and the farm buildings 500 metres across it, aren't actually part of The Patch itself, but they can be seen from The Patch, which means that every bird that occurs there goes on my Patch list. Not very discriminating, but everyone who watches a patch stretches his or her patch as much as possible; it's one of the rules of the game.

It was some months before we ventured further south, towards ground that has now become so familiar that it seems inconceivable that we were so reticent to explore it – although the fearsome fence no doubt played a part. It was in August 2002 that I first remember venturing down the public footpath between the western edge of The Lake and The Big Field. When I did, I discovered two things: a delightful water-filled ditch that was fringed by a few willow and oak trees; and the best place for abandoned cars and fly-tipping in the whole county, a hide-out for The Patch's small population of brown rats. Every patch has its eyesores and, despite the car wrecks providing refuge for wrens and probably wood mice, it is still something of a blot on the place.

Not so The Thicket, the small patch of trees now titled as such. I soon discovered that the water-filled ditch actually ran away some 600 metres to the west towards the next village, and south along the side of The Lake out of sight. A hedge (henceforth called The Hedge) followed the line of the ditch away to the west. Fringing the ditch either side was another field, about 0.4 of a hectare in extent. This was every birdwatcher's field of dreams, with some rough pasture, a few gnarled and unhappy hawthorns, and extremely wet edges grown up with enough species of waterside plants to fill a major herbarium. It's the home of whinchats, reed buntings and bank voles. I later discovered that this field floods in winter and plays host to horses in summer. The horses are large, horrendously inquisitive and completely intimidating. I suspect them of having eaten the last of the guard dog patrols. In honour of its fair season inhabitants it is called The Shire Field.

Later that autumn I first followed the unpaved road (The Lane) that now forms the northern boundary of The Patch, running from the edge of The Big Field to the big, busy 'A' Road that is overbearingly The Patch's eastern boundary, a distance of some 400 metres. Walking along here from the west, one at first follows hedges guarded by ferocious brambles, the secret spot where locals such as us bring the children to pick blackberries. There are a few houses along here, one of which used to be owned by a retired blacksmith, a friendly giant of a man who once worked for royalty and, I suspected, might have been able to bend metal with his hands if he found that his tools had failed to work. When I first walked The Patch he would always be ready with a friendly word, while at the same time, invariably, his dog took a friendly bite out of my leg. I began to run out of plasters. Further along, close to The 'A' Road itself, there are a few paddocks for horses on the southern side of The Lane. Here live equines that graze the days away quietly and are sometimes ridden. I frequently see their owners bringing them hay and, in contrast to the situation on The Shire Field, getting out alive afterwards.

For a couple of years I visited The Lake and farmland area mentioned above quite frequently and saw some excellent birds, such as little ringed plover and lesser whitethroat. Only in spring 2004 did it occur to me that it might be worth checking further south. This might seem a little unadventurous, but you must understand that there was a busy, dusty working quarry here next to The Lake, and it was about as attractive-looking as a multi-storey car park in a slum. I could see the dust rising from it from The Lane, and there was a constant rumble from lorries. It had all the appearance of a bird-free zone.

Only it wasn't. In April 2004 I ventured along the overgrown public footpath that ran south from the south-east corner of The Lake, carrying a machete, mosquito repellent and pens for any locals who might be enraged by my presence. After three or four days of hacking in the baking heat, I finally came out, eyes blinking, upon an area of fields flanked by the suburban houses that had grown up along The 'A' Road. By climbing over a low fence and following the edge of these fields I then found I could crawl through some prickly hawthorns and stinging nettles in order to get a view of The Quarry itself for the first time. It proved to be a delightful shock. Much was a waste ground of churned up mud and tyre tracks, but there was a great deal of scrub and weedy wilderness. There were even some shallow pools and small reed-beds, and through excited eyes it looked like a neighbourhood version of the RSPB reserve at Minsmere.

It didn't take long for some good birds to turn up here, such as dunlin and common tern, and it soon became apparent that The Quarry was Gull City. Hundreds of them used to perch or sit and loaf around on The Quarry's hallowed and greatly disturbed ground, occasionally bullying each other and making a lot of noise, rather like a chamber of politicians – and achieving roughly the same. Not everybody loves gulls, not even birdwatchers, but when they are one of the mainstays of your patch you find yourself drawn into that dark world that is inhabited by gull-watchers, and it is quite impossible to escape. Gulls have that same appeal that higher mathematics does: the sheer complicated nature of identifying them is quite attractive, and a quick dip of the toe will fool you into thinking that you have a chance of understanding it. Of course this never happens – the gull manuals will continue to gather dust next to your unread copy of *A Brief History of Time*. The gull-watcher's existence is a world where such utter trifles as leg colour, mantle colour, the length of the primary flight feathers and the lower cutting edge of the bill all assume an extraordinary significance, because they are necessary for identifying gulls to species, race, sex and very precise age. And who can resist toying with issues of age, race and sex?

At about the same time that I 'discovered' The Quarry, the real owners of my Patch, Bournemouth and West Hampshire Water, opened up The Lake to visitors. They didn't make a song and dance about it, but they put in a stile and mowed the edges, so that a true circumnavigation became possible. And because the banks were raised, this also offered a superb view over the adjoining fields and The Quarry itself. Not surprisingly, the whole area became a much better place for birds. I began to visit far more often, and made a point of collating records, including counts of all the ducks and gulls.

It was the appearance of one particular duck, a small brown and boring specimen, that heralded a subtle change in the birding scene of The Patch towards the end of the noughties. The duck happened to be a garganey, a very scarce bird that would delight any patch-watcher anywhere in Britain. It turned up one September as part of a large group of moulting ducks, and because The Lake was such a small water-body, this garganey acquired the habit of giving very good views. No matter that it was in its dullest plumage of the year and would barely register a raised eyebrow from a member of the public: it was a garganey and it was easy to see. For the first time in The Patch's life it began to attract a number of visiting bird-watchers. This included two other locals, Trevor Thorpe and Chris Parnell, whose obsession matched mine. We are all still birding here today and, for reasons that I shall come to, are being joined by an ever-growing band of co-enthusiasts.

It never occurred to me, over the years that I happily retraced a plod around and around The Lake, that there was a whole wodge of terrific habitat and countryside that had still eluded my eyes, even though it lay less than a hundred metres away from one of my regular haunts. I did know that there was a small ribbon of woodland across The River from The 'A' Road, but it never looked at the time as though it would amount to much. It was only a rather shameless attitude to list-keeping that forced me to consider a search of the area in 2007. You see, while the list of farmland, waterside and open country birds was pretty healthy and thriving, The Patch was not offering a decent supply of woodland birds. For a long time a nuthatch was as rare as an osprey. But maybe the aforementioned ribbon might hold a few woodland treasures to fill in some of the gaps?

The trouble was that this ribbon lay behind a gate into a small water treatment plant, which displayed signs warning about the terrible outcome of unauthorized access to the southern Quarry area. It seemed that, if the mythical guard dogs didn't get you, you were first and foremost likely to be crushed under the wheels of a quarry lorry; if you avoided the driving assassins and squeaked in you were almost certain to drown, be electrocuted, or quite possibly both. All in all, the impression given was that the public were not welcome in this particular part of Utilityland.

I'm not saying that the Water Company were unpleasant or restrictive (indeed, I have found them subsequently to be completely the opposite), but it wasn't easy to obtain permission to nose about. After twenty or more e-mails came and went with lukewarm encouragement, and then several phone calls produced similar messages of misgiving, a woman called Tina finally agreed to give me a tour of the area across The River. I think she just took pity on me, rather than succumbing to the offers of money, sex and free bird books that I tried.

Had I known what a delightful little Shangri-La actually lay behind the unpromising Water Company buildings, I would have bravely dodged lorries, deep pools and cables – and a lot more danger besides – to get there sooner. For a start, it was a much larger area than I had realized: what I now call The South Side actually constitutes a third of The Patch by area. And it was prime birding habitat. Working from the east and following The River, the buildings were adjacent to a large grassy field (where in the subsequent years, admittedly, I have seen precisely nothing), next to which was the ribbon of woodland that had originally aroused my curiosity. The wood, which I called Emily's Wood after my daughter, turned out to be a real mishmash of tree species, dominated by a number of tall poplars, which host summit meetings for carrion crows and provide holes for the sites of tawny owls. There were whole rafts of birches and alders, and some pretty serious understorey. It is something of a shattered and splintered wood, and its arboretum-like cast-list of species, which includes the only local horse chestnuts, a huge laurel and, who knows, probably a medlar and a mulberry, suggests that it has a long history of eccentric planting.

Along from Emily's Wood, The River flows quietly west for a short stretch and then convulses left and back round right, almost creating an island in the process. It was this area between the bends that most completely caused my eyes to pop out of my head on that memorable first visit with Tina. The reason – not a big one, not perfect, but nevertheless real – was a marsh that had formed where The River turned south. Marshes, you need to understand, make birdwatchers go weak at the knees, because they host a number of very special birds. The instant I saw it I imagined water rails, bitterns and bearded tits, here all in my Patch, a place that I had assumed was just a mixture of lake and farmland. The future looked glorious.

Just one new wood and one small marsh would have been enough to make any grown patch-watcher break down in tears of gratitude, but Tina's tour of The South Side wasn't yet over. The path led west towards a large, open area which had been allowed to run wild, and was a jumble of tall herbs growing at chest height. This was, and still is, The Patch's most obvious wilderness, albeit a 2-hectare one, and it gives the impression that no human feet have trodden over it since at least Neolithic times, or at least since the evil fairy put all the staff of Sleeping Beauty's castle into their slumber. It often floods in the winter, and even today I haven't unravelled much of its wildlife. If aliens were ever to land on these West Fields, their visit could easily pass by without a smidgeon of human contact.

My tour eventually reached the western side of The Patch, where The River turned to the north. It was hard not to feel a frisson of exclusivity at this point, deep in the most private corner of the Water Company's land, and a full kilometre from where mere mortals were allowed to walk. It was clear that very few passed this way, evidenced by the increasing thickness of the ground vegetation and a concomitant collapse of any recognizable path. The final delight was in discovering a second wood running alongside The River. While Emily's Wood was a fractured, species-rich melting-pot, this was a stand of hundred-year-old oaks, with some holly for an understorey. And this stand of trees, which I named Samuel's Wood in honour of my son, was where I knew that some of The Patch's seriously tree-loving birds would be found; indeed, a nuthatch called from the treetops as if to confirm the impression.

Having one-third of my Patch revealed to me in an afternoon after spending five years discovering the first two-thirds was an overwhelming experience. In the following days and months I didn't visit The South Side as often as you might expect. It was almost too much, and I tended to wander around in a daze. It was a little like living near Leicester Square and suddenly discovering that it is only part of a larger place called London. That exaggerates the point, but doesn't nullify it. It was also remarkably difficult to watch birds there, especially compared to the ease of watching ducks floating around on a lake and gulls standing around on gravel. And The South Side is big. It also faces the south-west, the direction of the prevailing wind.

That, then, is a short tour of my Patch. I have to admit, it is a pretty good one, and I hope you don't consider it beyond the experience of yours. Mine holds one very large disadvantage compared to many, though, that being that it is inland from the sea. Patches next to the sea are the kings of patches. They allow us to see more birds, it is easier to predict when the birds will be good, and there is usually an ice-cream van within easy reach.

But in a sense, I'm glad my Patch isn't by the sea and doesn't give me 200 species of birds a year. That's because I don't live near the sea, and so, with all its faults, The Patch is all I've got. That's another of the characteristics of patches: they are imperfect, and often let us down with their birds and other wildlife. When am I ever going to see an eider duck? The answer is never. But this helps me to appreciate everything that I am given, many times over. Patches aren't joyous because they overwhelm you with excitement and novelty – they are joyous because they help you to appreciate what you already have.

I mentioned earlier that patches change, and this applies very strongly to mine. This diary essentially covers the year 2009, apart from periodic backward and forward glances to special events, and even since then The Patch has undergone an evolution faster than that of a mutating fruit-fly. Where The Quarry once invited gulls on to its Elysian sand-bars there is now a very large and very deep lake or, as the Water Company persuades everyone to call it, a reservoir (fair enough, it is designed to wet the area's whistles in times of drought). This feature alone will add enormously to the area's attraction for birds. There are also two precious islands, now the very hub of bird activity for the whole site.

The nature of The Patch has changed in other ways. It was once possible to walk around it for three hours without seeing a soul, especially when the weather was inclement. Now such isolation is impossible. There is a Visitor Centre, with toilets (toilets!), there are anglers on The Lake, and now there are an increasing number of enthusiasts who go birding there. Quiet whispers have mentioned a hide in the future. Goodness knows, it might become a major birding site one day.

But I don't mind that. True, the year 2009 was the last of its kind but much as I feel affection for that birding year, life for The Patch moves onward and upward and more and more people are going to be delighting in its treasures from now on. I know I am lucky, because many patches degrade over time as they suffer from increased development and disturbance. But whatever happens, good or bad, that doesn't affect the relationship between any patch-watcher and their patch. Mine is still mine.

JANUARY

Thursday 1 January 2009

You've met The Patch, and so it's now high time we went birdwatching. And what better day to start than on 1 January itself, New Year's Day? Well, actually, there is a better date – 22 December. To wildlife this is far more important, because it is the day after the twenty-four hour period when there is least daylight and most darkness, and in many of our creatures, the shift in day length towards positive is marked by important biological changes. Hormonal systems are switched on for the first time round about 22 December, including sex hormones that prepare the creatures for breeding. One of the immediate results is that birds, for example, begin to sing vigorously. A large number of animals, including over-wintering insects and hibernating mammals, depend on the photoperiod, that one completely reliable natural clock, to tune their life-cycles correctly. Temperature and weather are merely fine-tuning parameters.

But anyway, we will start on 1 January, because it also marks an important date for us, the wildlife-watchers. We do tend to divide our wildlife experiences up into years. For example, in our gardens we will often declare to ourselves that it's been a good or bad year for butterflies, or that more goldfinches have visited the bird feeder this winter as opposed to last, or that it would be nice to see a brown hare this summer, having missed one last year. We might even make a greater effort in the early months to see some choice creature or plant that is special to us. I'm not sure why we do this; perhaps it comes from the farmer's or gardener's appreciation of how the natural cycles change, or perhaps it is simply because wildlife is outside, where the seasons are obvious. It would be interesting to know whether this appreciation of twelve-month cycles leaks over into other, more indoor or artificially based hobbies, such as train-spotting or needlecraft. Do train enthusiasts say: 'It's been a good year for locomotive class 37', I wonder?

Bird enthusiasts often get quite obsessed by what they see year on year, and go so far as to keep lists. And here I must admit that I am one of these. I enjoy ticking off the species that I see on The Patch every year. Why? Well, first it is fun and a challenge, and it keeps me going all through the year, especially if I am within sight of seeing more birds in a given twelve-month than the previous one. And second, it helps to keep the birdwatching experience fresh. It means that every single year, every one of the hundred-odd species I find will be 'new for the year' on one occasion. That amounts to a hundred satisfying encounters a year, even without the concomitant delights of being outside, seeing birds well and generally enjoying watching them. And this means that, for one day at least, even the most common species will deserve that title.

Keen patch-watchers almost invariably keep these lists, and as a result, not surprisingly, they enjoy going birding on 1 January a great deal. That is the day when they will see more birds new for the year than any other. And of course, the silly thing about it – as every patch-watcher will acknowledge – is that only yesterday the very same birds were infinitely less significant.

Anyway, having attempted to justify this eccentricity, I am about to take you on my 1 January 2009 birding trip, during which we will see some of The Patch's bread and butter birds.

For those who find the listing bit incomprehensible, fear not. As we go, I will assuage your alarm by attempting to flavour the encounters with some choice intrigue about each species that we find.

As I park along The Lane and prepare to cast my eyes over The Lake for the first time in 2009, I speculate on what might be my first species of the year. It's always fun to start with a good one: a jolt of blue from a kingfisher, perhaps, or a formation-flock of royal mute swans making their way regally over the cherished airspace by means of their slow, majestic wing-beats, their snow-white plumage glinting in the sun.

Well, no, actually, it's a lesser black-backed gull. And it's a grotty view of an adult disappearing into the distance above The Lake, just visible against the grey, moist sky of a dull January morning. It's the ornithological equivalent of getting a tax bill in the post when you were hoping for a birthday card.

No matter. Even a lesser black-backed gull is special in its way. Forty years ago it would have been noteworthy to see this species any time during the winter in southern England, let alone on 1 January. Forty years ago the lesser black-backed gull was almost as much a confirmed summer visitor to Britain as a swallow.

My second species is another gull, the black-headed gull, and at risk of you, the reader, fearing that a vast treatise on British gulls will follow on these pages, I can assure you that it won't be so. The black-headed gull is one of those species of British birds that has been saddled with a ridiculous name that has somehow stuck, in the same hall of shame as the grey wagtail (which is primarily yellow) and the bearded tit (which happens not to have a beard, and is not technically a tit at all). It so happens that, at no time in its life, does this gull have a black head – misleading, eh? In the winter, as now, it has no more than a speck of dark behind and above its eye, and in the summertime it has an undoubtedly fine, but very much dark chocolate brown, hood. The baffling name isn't easily explained, but it might be that it is derived from a time when people did not customarily distinguish between black and brown. After all, much the same blinkers, if you'll pardon the pun, seem to have been worn by those who gave the technical names for the colours of horses.

The black-headed gull is almost the ultimate bread and butter bird at The Patch. It is one of the few species that can be found here every day of the year, and it also holds the record for the largest flock of anything to have graced this hallowed ground – 463 birds. And remarkably, not a single one of these individuals is ever invited. Quite the reverse; the gulls are actively discouraged here, because The Patch lies under the flight-path of a medium-sized airport. Every time a plane is about to arrive or depart, a recording of a gull in distress is broadcast over a loudspeaker to the assembled throng of white bodies, who proceed to ignore it completely, and carry on bathing, bickering, loafing and metaphorically chewing gum, as is their wont. It makes no difference to anything, except for being irritating to hear. And the truly daft part is that, if the gulls actually reacted to the bird-scarer by taking off and flying around in panic, this might make them *more* liable to enter into the airspace used by the planes. It's the sort of idea that can only have been hit upon by a man wearing a suit and smart shoes who once found his shoulders splattered by gull poo.

If the authorities really wanted to keep birds away from The Patch, they should perhaps have considered using the distress calls of members of the crow family as well as gulls, for crows, rooks and jackdaws often outnumber the white pieces in this outdoor game of chess. This morning it is the rooks, with their soiled white faces and odd pointed bills, that make an appearance first, quickly followed by the smaller, faster-flapping jackdaws, both species passing over in small parties. To some extent both these birds betray the relatively rural aspect of The Patch, because rooks, in particular, need an admixture of tall trees and wide open, productive fields in order to thrive. Rooks don't breed on-site, but they make regular flights over, especially early in the morning and late in the evening, when several hundred may pass in mass commuting movements no different from the human to and fro movements going on below along The 'A' Road. The predictable, straight-line flights of rooks from colony to feeding grounds are what give rise to the expression 'as the crow flies'. The expression dates from mediaeval times, when bird flight-lines were part of the fabric of rural life, seemingly as dependable as sunrise and sunset and genuinely part of everyday conversation, while the differentiation between these two very similar large black birds was neither easy nor relevant. (Along the same lines, it so happens that 'scarecrows' were actually designed to frighten highly sociable rooks as opposed to more solitary crows.) Many birdwatchers, even armed with modern binoculars, still find rooks and their blacker, more sinister relatives the carrion crows hard to distinguish today.

In The Hedge beside The Lake appear three small brown bird species, one after the other, each one famous for the sort of behaviour that would suit the front page of a tabloid. Two, the dunnock and wren, are famous for their sex lives, while the robin is basically a thug. We all know that robins are cute in appearance, and spend at least some of the winter perching on spades, with their plumage fluffed up, looking doe-eyed and harmless. Yet these birds also have a capacity for astonishing violence, and in the autumn and spring, when territorial battles flare, robins quite frequently kill each other.

Meanwhile, the fruity behaviour of the other two species is less obvious, but intriguing. The female wren, for example, is notable for taking as much interest in a male's property as the male himself; males build up to five nests in their territory, and when a female is thinking of pairing up, she essentially takes a tour of the nests to see whether the male is up to standard. The male, meanwhile, frequently attracts more than a single female to pair up with himself and his portfolio, so becoming bigamous. But compared to the dunnock, this bigamy is child's play. Dunnocks are frequently bigamous, especially the females, but what sets the dunnock apart is that a male and female paired to each other can both be bigamous, or more, at the same time. In other words, a single female, for example, might pair up with anything up to three male mates, while at the same time she might have to share them all with another female. I am told that, in certain places, this simply mirrors life in a student hall of residence.

Amongst the most controversial birds at The Patch, or at least one that seems to inflame and divide opinion more than most, here and everywhere, is the cormorant. These birds live semi-permanently within our area, not so much in The Lake or River itself as upon a couple of pylons that loom over Samuel's Wood. The birds, up to sixty of them in all, gather on the metal branches and on the wires and seem to do nothing much all day except for breaking into the occasional communal gurgle, like a group of politicians murmuring 'Hear, hear!' at a debate. Cormorants, remarkably, only need about half an hour twice a day to feed themselves if pickings are good, so the rest of their time is their own. They perch, preen and hold out their wings open to dry – in an attitude that looks irresistibly like a declaration that the last fish they caught was 'this big'.

It is, of course, the anglers who find cormorants bothersome, and this is a subject to which I shall return. Anglers are as much a part of The Patch as their nemeses and, as a detached and often bemused observer, I find that the biology of both parties is extraordinarily analogous. Think of this: each sits around all day seemingly doing nothing, with the occasional grunting grumble forming the main means of communication, and the brightest spots in their lives involve brief moments when they catch fish. The two constituencies are made for each other.

The Patch is at heart a wetland, and New Year's Day brings the usual decent selection of water-loving birds, including the ever-present coots. Try as I might, I find it hard to summon up much enthusiasm for coots, despite their peculiar appearance, superficially duck-like but with the most extraordinary lobed, bluish feet that would not look out of place on the legs of a fantasy monster from a space movie. Coots are coal-black with a bright white shield above the bill – also white, faintly tinted with pink – and in theory they should be quite handsome, but somehow they are not. Perhaps their temperament, which is irascible and prickly, and the sounds that they make, which are somehow unnecessarily loud and a touch discordant, let them down. They just don't light up The Patch, and their constant bickering is tiresome rather than interesting. The thing is, they aren't like robins, professional and pretty assassins that do violence properly; instead they are just disagreeable and a bit amateurish.

The rest of the waterbirds mill over The Lake's waters under the soberly clad winter sky, and since they are all reasonably undisturbed, I have a go at counting them, a process that I find strangely satisfying. To go birding and records each species is a pleasure; but to go birding and make an accurate count, that feels like science. The totals mean something, and they can contribute to similar spot-counts that take place at the same time all over the country. Every winter the British Trust for Ornithology runs a Wetland Bird Survey (WEBS) to which amateurs are invited to contribute their numbers.

Anyway, today's count reveals a respectable mix of ducks, including forty tufted ducks and thirty-two mallards, species that would be expected on most moderately sized freshwater lakes in southern England. More pleasingly, there are also thirty-four gadwalls here today. These are underrated ducks in every sense. At first sight or at a distance, with their subdued colours, the males cannot be compared flatteringly to their gaudy counter-parts such as mallards or teal. Yet close up they are like a pastel masterpiece, their grey breast patterned by dense scallops and their undersides tightly vermiculated, the whole topped off with soft red-brown, black-striped plumes that drape over their wings.

A squared-off white panel is formed by the inner trailing feathers of the wing, which shows as a spot in the middle of the wing, and they also have yellow-orange legs. With a thin, very straight neck and rounded crown, they swim around with an appealing regal air, in complete contrast to the flat-crowned mallards, commoners to the core.

You wouldn't expect a gadwall to hurt a fly – and indeed, these are the most vegetarian of ducks, whose ducklings buck the generic trend of subsisting on midges when they first hatch – but in fact they have a bullying side, and the object of their persecution is a surprising one, the coot. Coots and gadwalls eat much the same thing, plant material, but the difference is that coots, by diving to the bottom of any given shallow body of water, can reach more of it than gadwalls, which are surface-feeders. Unfortunately, coots cannot swallow underwater, and the sight of a coot surfacing with a bounteous blob of pondweed is too tempting for your average gadwall to bear. Armed with greater bodily bulk than a coot, the gadwall intim-idates its rival into giving up its hard-earned meal. And of course, once any individual swims down this alley, it is hard to go back, and there are records of gadwalls subsisting for months, literally, on this ill-gotten gain. Yet when you see gadwalls and coots floating around together on the water, it is hard to appreciate the surface tension.

There are other notable ducks around today, too, including shovelers, pochards, teals and wigeons, but you will hear plenty more about these later on. The Patch is also a respectable site for their swimming colleagues, the grebes, which as far as the aquatic life is concerned, make ducks and other wildfowl look like weekend hobbyists. With legs set so far back on the body that they are almost left behind, and with lobed toes that move around at the foot joint (actually the metatarsal) in all direc-tions, grebes are more or less useless on land, a bit like feathered seals, and they hardly ever haul up for anything except to build a nest, incubate and, weirdly, copulate. In the water, however, with their powerful flipper-like feet and stream-lined bodies, they are fast and manoeuvrable, proving what a different world lurks under the surface of any freshwater lake.

Today, unusually, our small species, the little grebe, outnumbers its big cousin, the great crested grebe, as it happens by seven individuals to one. Local great cresteds from The Patch almost certainly go to sea for the winter, where they can tolerate much larger waves and currents than their diminutive counterparts. The weedy little grebes, also known as dabchicks (or originally dip-chicks, because of their frequent diving), float about instead in the calm waters, where they feed on small fish and insect larvae. When loafing they often allow their plumage to ruffle, especially their raised rear ends, the cotton-like down giving them the appearance of rabbits taking a swim.

Most trips to The Patch reveal something out of the ordinary, and today's unexpected bird happens to be a snipe, flushed by something from the bowels of The Quarry. Snipe are cryptically coloured stripy brown waders with inordinately long, straight bills with which they probe into soft mud for a living. Most of the time they keep hidden on the ground, but when disturbed they have two speeds of flight, fast and very fast, and always seem to be completely panicked and out of control. They take off at full throttle, alarm-calling a sound that resembles a quick but undeniably passionate kiss, and then tear hither and thither in madcap, zigzagging fashion, often circling around an area dozens of times before finally landing. This highly strung behaviour is in complete contrast to their demeanour on the ground; the moment their feet touch the mud, they go into slow motion, creeping guiltily forward as if embarrassed about what has gone before.

Snipe are scarce at The Patch, with just a few individuals over-wintering, and they are so secretive that they are not often seen. This, therefore, is the bird of the day, alongside what is a very familiar supporting cast. Besides the ones I have mentioned, there are other species that find their way on to the New Year list, birds such as collared doves and grey herons, starlings and blue tits. By the end of the trip I have catalogued thirty-six species in an hour or so, which is about average for here.

Yet however average this particular visit turned out to be, and however many times I have seen all of today's species on The Patch before, the new-for-the-year moment for each one was actually quite special on this day. It's a strange quirk of the turn of the year, when what is familiar glints, albeit temporarily, with novelty and promise.

Monday 5 January 2009

Every year brings something special, and this year the something special has arrived with inordinate haste. A flurry of north-easterlies has brought a cold snap and a late Christmas present.

I arrive at The Patch before it is fully light, hoping that the birds reported yesterday are still there. The prospect of missing them gnaws as uncomfortably as the searing cold. This morning the frost weighs heavily, covering the ground with a soft bluish-white carpet, interrupted by the defiant green of clumps of taller herbs such as docks and nettles. The leafless trees on the edge of The Shire Field are stark against the sky, which lightens stubbornly, black fingers sticking out into dark grey, then slate grey, then smoky grey. The waters of The Lake loll uninterestedly, coldly lapping the banks, and the reeds around the edge are studded with frost crystals. I edge along the western shore, my breath shooting steam. I feel like a freak of heat in a relentlessly frigid landscape.

The first scan of The Shire Field and of the fields by The River draws a blank. The grassland is empty. With a telescope I check fields progressively further away, checking them corner by corner, but still there isn't any movement. I begin to curse the fact that I wasn't here yesterday evening.

Soon, though, there is a sound from Canada geese in the

distance, from the far side of The Quarry. Normally, these birds' broken-voiced, dissonant, hiccupping honks are part of the unappreciated soundscape of The Patch, disliked along with the gull-scarers and The 'A' Road traffic. But today I hear them and my heart lifts. The flock comes directly towards me and heads for the fields. Has a flock of Canada geese ever been so welcome?

Yet of course, it's not the Canada geese that are welcome, but what they could be bringing with them. It's like watching a chat show on TV with a host you normally avoid, but who has a guest with star quality. Mind you, when the geese first fly past I cannot actually make out any guests, and when the birds finally land just out of sight, concealed by The Thicket, I must make a quick scramble over the crusted ground to get a decent look at the grazing birds.

And there they are, right at the extreme end of the group of forty-five Canadas: eight magical, gloriously wild white-fronted geese plus, as it happens, a single bonus greylag goose, which is also rare here. The white-fronted geese are considerably smaller and mousier-brown than their Canadian kin, with shorter necks. They are slightly detached from the carrying flock as well, keeping strictly together. The bond with their hosts is expedient and weak.

The light is poor and the birds are hunkered down, but it is still possible to make out their signature feature, the white noseband at the base of their bills. It hardly qualifies as much of a 'white front', and many consider the name misleading; but in fact it comes from the French *front*, which means 'forehead', and is thus perfectly appropriate. And of course, when the geese are flying along with their necks outstretched, the white forehead is very much the first thing that the watcher sees.

Not quite all the geese in front of me have the hallmark feature; one bird has the merest pencil-thin line of white between the bill and face, confirming it as a young bird. Six months ago it was an egg, and now it is a bright-eyed, fit, well-travelled young goose, treading a field in southern England having hatched somewhere in the vastness of the Russian tundra. It has grown up under the nurture of one of the best support systems of any British bird. Not only has it had the good fortune to follow its mother and father on migration, and thus been excused the burden of finding its own way south, but this individual will also enjoy a gentle first winter season under the strict protection of its extended family. Its father and mother will commission every patch of grazing ground they walk on as a temporary territory, keeping other families off, and the young-ster will feed without too many distractions. And remarkably, the next winter it will again associate in a similar way with parents and siblings, and even for the winter after that. White-fronted geese are probably unique among British birds for the extended period of care that they offer to their young, albeit only in the non-breeding season.

Thus, life for this young goose is relatively cushy – if feeding on ice-cold fields in the open air can be called cushy.

My suspicions about the Russians' lack of cosiness with their New World colleagues proved to be well founded. The following morning they were gone and they never returned. Wherever they went I shall never know, but somehow I suspect that their heart lay to the east.

Great Birding Days

Thursday 7 January 2010

It is a curious and sobering fact that the very best and most exciting days for birdwatching can often be the very worst of days for the birds themselves. Today was such a day. There was much suffering and confusion. As an observer, I was utterly unable to help the birds I was watching, yet I was left with a guilty feeling for taking pleasure, in the form of wonder and excitement, in being one of the witnesses to a major event.

The winter of 2009/2010 proved to be the fiercest in Britain for about fifty years, and 7 January was one of its defining days. It was a day when, despite being covered in snow, the countryside looked colourless and bleak. Here in southern England, snow is usually such a novelty that its presence adds a thrill and enchantment. But by this time, after weeks of cold and many falls, the landscape wore the snow as its workaday clothes. It lay in ugly patches and had lost all its glamour. Even my children had begun to decline the offer of sledging and snowball fights.

The cold was beginning to take its toll on birds near and far. At home, the long nights were claiming thousands of small deaths at a time; birds that could not manage to build up enough fat reserves to get them through to dawn, and so succumbed from cold-induced starvation. Theirs was a bloodless death of fading away, a fire gradually going out; there were no witnesses in the darkness. In normal circumstances they would have been missed in the usual roll-call of living birds; a vacancy in a territory here or within a hierarchy there. But in the snow- and frost-induced crisis, when birds were travelling here and there in increasingly desperate searches for food, even their passing was lost. Birders didn't notice. Feeders in gardens were double- and treble-booked, by outsiders as well as residents, and the apparently healthy figures were distorted by the abnormality of the situation. Healthy figures masked the lack of credit among garden birds.

Far away there was a different effect. The cold weather was producing refugees. When harsh conditions strike, birds can stay put and try to ride out the difficulties. But equally, if they find conditions suddenly untenable, they can evacuate from an area and move in the hope of finding sustainable conditions elsewhere. On the Continent, where frost and snow are basic ingredients for the winter, quite a few species do this, and by nature they tend to fly in a westerly or southerly direction, often turning up in Britain. However, in case such movements sound planned and tame, be assured that they arise out of danger and chaos. Human refugees move when things are desperate; they usually move on a whim and have no time to pack. For birds it is the same, and not for nothing are their evacuations known as 'escape movements'.

Mass escape movements are a rare sight in Britain. They don't occur every winter, and it is unpredictable as to when and where they do occur. To witness one, though, can sear the birding memory. When I was a child I remember being spell-bound by accounts from the desperately bitter winter of 1962/63, when Britain was covered in snow between November and March. Some observers, braving snowstorms and extreme cold, spoke of the thousands of birds that they witnessed streaming purposefully over, hour after hour, and this over perfectly ordinary parts of Britain, not at well known migration watch-points where one might expect large movements to occur. Strange birds turned up everywhere, even in people's back gardens. Some migrants dropped dead out of the sky. There was a potent clash of meteorological and ornithological extremes. For months no birder knew what the next day would bring in terms of either, except that neither would be ordinary. It was desperate and sad, but compelling. Birders didn't want to see it happen, but, if you understand the paradox, if it was happening, they wanted to see it.

And if you'll forgive the apparent indifference towards the birds, I had always wanted to see a major escape movement. In the same way, despite the destructive and sometimes tragic power of a tornado, I would still like to see one. On this day, 7 January, I finally connected with the former.

Nothing happened on the epic scale of the events of fifty years ago that I have mentioned. I did not have to fight snowdrifts to get to The Patch, and no flocks of birds darkened the skies. Instead there wasn't a whiff of romance. It was all a little cold and clinical. However, from the moment that I saw a small, disorganized flock of fieldfares passing over from the car park, it was obvious that something was going on. Before I had assumed the ten layers of clothing I needed to cope with the cold, several similar flocks had appeared against the lightening skies.

Fieldfares are classic exponents of escape movements. Although they are essentially northern birds, breeding in the woodlands of Scandinavia, they don't cope well with hardship. In common with many winter refugees they are ground feeders, digging for worms and leatherjackets, and when the frost hardens the surface of pasture, they are frozen out. And just as frost strikes overnight, so fieldfares must sometimes evacuate with indecent haste in order to survive. Who knows from where these individuals took off this morning, in the unimaginable cold of the pre-dawn?

I trudged gingerly on to the causeway between The Lake and The Quarry, and more fieldfares bustled by. These large members of the thrush family, with their attractive combination of black tail, smoky grey head and rump and glorious velvet-purple back, don't fly like normal birds. They flap their wings in a weirdly haphazard, stop-start, casual manner, and their flocks seem incapable of keeping together. A typical fieldfare flock at a distance looks like a bundle of autumn leaves caught by an unexpected gust of wind. Today, though, flying into the cold northerly, some of this effect had been lost, although the flocks still weren't as coherent as those of most birds. And the groups were small. Instead of the multitudes one might expect in an escape movement, the birds today were going over in streams, maybe ten or twenty at a time.

Very soon I disturbed a party of quite different birds that had settled on the grassy edge of The Quarry: as they rose they seemed to hover slightly, and gave off a familiar chirruping call. These were skylarks, another classic winter refugee. There were about twenty of them altogether, the most The Patch had ever hosted in a day. Normally, if you flush a flock of skylarks they will move away without too much ceremony and settle back to feeding perhaps fifty metres ahead. These birds, however, rose into the air and flew north over The Lake, into the wind and away: still travelling, still escaping.

As I watched these skylarks go, I heard the same call again, looked behind me and saw another party pass over, hot on the heels of the first. Within a minute or so another group, also of twenty birds, had done the same. Then came another flock of fieldfares, and by now it was quite obvious that the birds were all moving north, into the wind, at a height of between two and five metres above ground. Flocks of birds were appearing at the rate of about one every minute or so, but sometimes in waves, with several parties almost at once, with a longer gap in between. Predictably enough, redwings, close relatives of the fieldfares both genetically and ecologically, were also mixed in, as were a few song thrushes. Much higher up, a glint in the sky revealed a small group of golden plovers, slim and quick with rapid wing-beats, their underwings pure white; later a lanky, long-legged black-tailed godwit, another bird that forages over pasture, also followed along the invisible trail north. None of these were entirely 'normal' winter birds at The Patch, at least not in quantity. They were all transients, escapees.

But some birds, it seemed, had lost the will to escape. A few lapwings, wading birds with wispy crests, white bellies and iridescent green and purple backs, were standing still by the side of the frozen Quarry. Several were allowing far too close an approach for such shy and flighty birds. Only when I was three or four metres away would they tiptoe away, and then would not go far. If they did fly, they soon flopped down again. One was limping. These birds should have been part of the evacuating stream, up in the sky with the fieldfares and skylarks and plovers, but it seemed they were too exhausted or shell-shocked to move. Most would be dead within a few hours.

And what of the others? Before speculating on their fate, let us muse a little on the scale of the movement. In an hour of watching, I counted more than two hundred fieldfares and the same number of redwings, but many, many passed without being logged because they were all travelling fast and were passing on a broad front, so that flocks passing a hundred or so metres away could easily be missed. I also counted 235 Skylarks in the hour; extraordinary not for the actual number, but for the skylarks' history at The Patch – ten individuals was the previous day record, now exceeded more than twenty-fold, and that in just an hour. More than a thousand would have moved over in the course of a morning, and who knows how many thrushes did? Three thousand? Five thousand? Up in the air, on the busy refugees' road, numbers would easily have become distorted or lost.

Taking a conservative figure, I estimate that at least six thousand birds would have passed over The Patch on the morning of 7 January 2010. That, of course, was just The Patch, a pinprick in the frozen countryside. Clearly, the overall movement, even just in southern England, was huge. Therefore, when we consider what happened to all these birds, the sheer number of lives involved makes the speculation sobering and emotional. Remember, first of all, that the movement was northerly. At first this seems baffling. Then, as a birder, I recall that most migrating birds prefer to move into the wind (it helps with lift), so long as it isn't too strong. Today's wind was biting, northerly, but manageable. Yet then I am baffled again. Most escape movements take birds in a south-westerly direction. So why was everything moving north?

This is where speculation makes the blood run cold. Perhaps these birds had all flown south-west and, finding frost and snow cover everywhere, were now turning back? If so, they might have been using the lifting wind in an attempt to fly out of trouble. But ahead to the north lay a great deal more snow, frost and ice, and it is hard not to imagine that the weaker birds, perhaps thousands of them, were merely 'escaping' to their deaths. Perhaps they were now confused as well as weakened.

In the hour that I watched the temperature never rose above –9 °C, and the temperatures didn't relent much until several days later. Sooner or later, the flying refugees must have landed that day. Who knows where? And what happened to them all? Sometimes it is best not to know.

Sunday 25 January 2009

The month of January is following its usual birding course. By now I have seen seventy or so species at The Patch, and the new-for-year encounters are diminishing by the day. By the end of January, most birding encounters will be steeped in ordinariness and familiarity, just as the rhythm of everyday life, no longer stirred by resolutions for revolutions, has settled back into the same. Starved of repeated novelty, the patch-watcher must now take something from the ordinariness and from watching cycles turn. With careful monitoring, familiar things begin to betray patterns, and the patterns create under-standing. And the understanding of one's local patch is one of birding's great aims and treasures.

We are back into normal January weather-wise, too. There have been no more snowfalls to bring wild geese from Russia. It is the usual chilly-without-being-cold January, where nothing is exceptional and nothing is desperate. It is the waiting-for-the-spring January, that time of the year when the season begins to lose its sting and the cold is a chore rather than a terror. It's the time to watch the countryside for things that distract us from the present; to take our eyes off the leaden skies and look for early flowers in the frosty ground. Early spring flowers are no more attractive than late spring flowers such as cow parsley or hawthorn; it is what they predict that makes them special. Violets flower right into the depths of spring, and become upstaged by the day. Only in January or February do they lift our spirits.

Every patch has its downsides, and I've already said that a patch close to the sea is best for birds, while mine is embedded resolutely inland. Similarly, I would really enjoy a patch that provides a decent showing of spring flowers, but mine doesn't. Neither of the woods has a planting of snowdrops, let alone bluebells, and the only snowdrops present on-site are in the gardens by The East Fields, where they are surrounded by children's slides and trampolines and by bags of compost, and somehow just don't speak for the countryside at large. We have no crocuses either, and precious little early blossom. Although there are a few celandines and violets, there are no carpets of them. By the time the daffodils appear, mostly in the grounds of the pumping station, the secret of spring is already out and we hardly need to look for proof.

To anybody familiar with the outdoors, the most effective natural accomplice to very early spring-wishing is the increase in birdsong. Today Emily's Wood resounds to bird-speak, even on a walk taken in the middle of the morning. I have already mentioned that day-length rather than weather sets it off, and its increase, day on day, is irresistible, so that even by mid-January there is a serious chorus involving a good number of species. Just as spring flowers write colourful graffiti over the official sign saying 'winter', so birdsong drowns out its broadcast message.

No bird challenges and taunts winter so much as the great tit. It will sing robustly in the very early days of the year, and I have heard it on mornings when the temperature is five below and it is still dark. The song is a simple chime of two notes repeated several times, and it sounds something like 'teacher, teacher, teacher'. It is the simplicity and sheer cheerfulness that makes it so redolent of spring. Great tits are at their most resplendent at this time of the year, too, with brilliant yellow breasts, bold black stripes and blue wings. And this, in such contrast to the dull-hued season, makes this small creature a living embodiment of seasonal change.

It isn't the only singer, though. Up in Emily's Wood's willows and poplars blue tits have begun performing, but they have such a varied vocabulary that they never quite manage to sing away the blues as great tits do. Even so, they are soon a dominant sound, along with robins, which have changed their songs from those that accompanied the countryside's descent into autumn. From September onwards they sing a territorial effort that has long, rambling phrases that capture the melancholy of the season; but in December or January they switch to a different set of phrases that sound unmistakably more upbeat, and are sung from higher up in the trees. Meanwhile, mornings begin to be dominated by proclamations from song thrushes, and those undercover paeans to sauciness, the dunnocks, also begin their cyclical warbles – much more about them later. All in all, January days are noisily indifferent to the prevailing gloom, for those who are prepared to listen.

FEBRUARY

Monday 2 February 2009

So much for birdsong proclaiming the dominance of spring! Last night there was a north-east wind which brought the weather straight down again from Russia. It dumped five centimetres of snow. Having appreciated the white-fronted geese brought in by the last snowfall, I had high hopes for a trip to The Lake today. Surely something ornithological has been dumped as well?

The Patch was appropriately cold and wind-blasted, but at first the birds seemed to be stubbornly unaffected. The ducks just bobbed around on the unfrozen water as they do every day of the winter, occasionally raising their heads mid-slumber and giving a contemptuous glance in my direction as if to say: 'Oh, you again.'

Normally duck numbers change in bad weather. For example, anything well below freezing should usher mallards out from any ditches, puddles and reedy hollows where they normally hang out, for the simple reason that the water in such private refuges freezes and forces the wildfowl to the larger wetlands. But today there are only fourteen mallards on The Lake. Admittedly, this number has risen from only three a couple of days ago, but that is hardly evidence of a massive freeze-inspired exodus. And the numbers of tufted ducks and pochards were up by two birds and one bird respectively. Sometimes, birds really do make a fool of you.

The most exciting snow-inspired movement was – now, don't laugh – a flock of woodpigeons. There were eighty-four of them feeding on The Shire Field, and that is a serious-sized flock for my Patch. They were acting strangely, too. None of them seemed able to get settled. Every few moments one or more would take off, fly for a couple of metres and then land again, as if they were overweight grey butterflies flitting from flower to flower. Whenever they did land they seemed to feed prodigiously, although there seemed nothing to take but grass. It isn't clear why they were so fidgety, but the gusting wind could have been a factor, or perhaps there were too many trying to fit into a single space. Woodpigeons are notoriously protective of their personal space, and operate a ruthless social hierarchy. Those of lower status, which usually means the youngest birds, are forced by means of a rolling set of aggressive encounters on to the periphery of any feeding group, and here they remain until they can begin to win the odd scrap. Exclusion to the flock margins is dangerous, because they are far more exposed to predators (such as foxes or sparrowhawks) than are any birds that bask in the middle of the gathering. As a result, the youngsters spend a great deal of time glancing nervously around, lifting their heads when they should be feeding. Their weight drops and they become weaker, and ever more vulnerable. Many don't survive.

I can only guess that this flock may have formed in response to the snowy conditions, so perhaps the hierarchies were still in the process of being worked out, with birds being kicked off the grass every few seconds by hot-headed rivals. These are tiny battles, small instants of rejection that, put together, can sap the life from downtrodden individuals, incrementally fatal.

Meanwhile, to an observer it is intriguing to see and try to interpret behaviour like this. And I couldn't help musing: here am I, wandering around in −6 °C and the best thing I can see is a few pigeons – and yet I am absurdly grateful to them – excited even. Surely only patch-watchers can get truly inspired by such daily trifles.

There's also something about frost and snow that makes woodpigeons look unusually magnificent. No, seriously, they do. You'd never paint a pigeon in primary colours, of course, but here on this pastel-grey February afternoon, they are studies in subtle grey, white and pink, in perfect keeping with their surroundings. Despite their scruffy reputation, in the lean days of winter woodpigeons are invariably immaculate and smoothly-plumaged, and when they make quick take-offs, as they are doing today, the white wing-bands flicker the tired arena of sodden green grass and dishevelled snow-patches into life.

Yet, in the end, amidst a celebration of the most ordinary of birds, the visit does deliver something truly special, as a day with such extreme conditions always should. It delivers its gift to a backdrop of an upturn in snowfall, almost a white-out. Against the strengthening storm, a shape battles its way in from the west, and as soon as it catches my eye I can tell that it is special, the way it flies purposefully forward, the flaps subtly more powerful than anything I have been watching. It's obviously a small bird of prey, and the combination of sharp pointed wings and short tail identify it as a merlin. Merlins are usually described as dashing birds, but there's no dashing about for this individual today, not into this enthusiastic wind.

It flies straight past me and lands on a tall *leylandii* cypress on the edge of The Patch, a tree that has never previously been touched by celebrity talons, so far as I am aware. Through the flakes I can appreciate that it is a male, with a bluish-grey back and warm buff colour underneath; in contrast to other raptors there is barely a hint of a moustache, or other head pattern. The identification is satisfyingly certain; the circumstances satisfyingly extreme.

It is only the second merlin I have ever seen at The Patch, after a bird raced over one October a few years ago, as hastening and preoccupied as a city cyclist on his way to work. And while the odd merlin might be expected to pass through in autumn, this midwinter bird is a real surprise. They do wander widely at such times, but most individuals stay on the coast, where they live on small birds.

Perhaps the snow forced this bird away from its usual haunts and brought it here as a step on its journey. Somehow, I doubt it. Northern birds like this should not be fazed by the odd spot of arctic weather. Just ask the ducks.

Tuesday 3 February 2009

The night is cold and crisp and holds a certain promise. There is adventure to be had, even close to home, in taking an hour out from a frosty evening to wrap up warm, shun the comforts and creep around in the darkness.

Ostensibly, this is a trip to see, or hear, whether any owls occur on The Patch – in the years I have watched, I have never encountered a single one here. But its real purpose is to add a little frisson to life. So I am taking a short walk in the dark, in February, in freezing conditions, close to a perilously deep and cold river. It isn't much of a risk, but it isn't *EastEnders*.

The night has been blessed with a satisfyingly drenching dark, the sort of dark that is so close and personal that it makes me feel that, if I shook my hands hard enough, some of it might fall in splodges to the ground. It is a night where eyesight can only make suggestions. I have decided to approach Emily's Wood from the overgrown field on the opposite side of The River to it, and see whether an owl calls. It is a place where I have never walked, and there is something deliciously perverse about doing it now when I cannot see anything except some distant houses in front and the lights of The 'A' Road behind.

In truth, I don't get far. But it doesn't matter in conditions like this. Night and cold make it easier to plunge into dislocation from what you are used to, and the short distance is enough: I am alone with the wildlife.

Almost immediately there is a loud, sharp 'ke-wick' from the depths of Emily's Wood. It is made by a tawny owl, proving that this species does occur here. I cannot see it, but the call alone reveals that this is the incumbent. Tawnies are among the most sedentary of all British birds, so that once they settle on a territory, they never leave it for the rest of their lives. Night by night they reconnoitre every corner, learning by trial and error which parts are good for hunting, and which areas bear fruit in different weather conditions. They learn where to shelter in a west wind, and discover where mice will venture out when it is raining. They will soon adopt favourite hunting perches, where they feel sharp-witted and comfortable. They will keep intruders away, with shocking violence if necessary. Single owls will hope to attract a mate, and thereby they will settle into a routine where they might easily outlast their human neighbours. It isn't unusual for a tawny owl to occupy a street or park for ten years or more, plenty of time for the human population to come and go.

Incidentally, many people think that the males hoot and only the female tawnies go 'ke-wick' in reply. In fact, this is the universal call, used by both sexes at any time of year; a sort of tawny owl conversation. So, although there is a territorial owl here, I cannot tell whether it is male or female, paired or unpaired.

The tawny owl's arresting 'ke-wick' is not the only call of the night. Almost immediately there is the triple bark of a fox, another slightly eerie noise that you can often hear on the soundtrack of a creepy film. Although a dog's more fulsome bark can be intimidating, it tends to be very direct and 'in your face'. On the other hand, there is something unnerving about the fox's call. It's an understated signal with a slightly melancholy tone, menacing rather than frightening. It suits the darkness perfectly.

The call is probably made by a dog fox. We are now at the end of the fox's rutting season, and the dog's job is to follow his mate around to keep her honest. A vixen is only in oestrus for three weeks of the year, and it is thought that she is possibly only actually fertile for three days altogether. That means that the male needs to be exceptionally attentive, to make sure that he fertilizes the female enough to produce a litter, and to make sure that another male doesn't slip in when he is not looking. There are many records of litters with more than one father.

After a few moments the fox does actually appear, close to The 'A' Road in the glow of the street lights. And, lo and behold, the vixen materializes shortly afterwards, her face close to the ground. Both lope away into the thick vegetation. The dog fox is doing his job for now, it seems. The next triple bark hails from much further off in the distance.

Once the short concert is over, the evening brings no more excitement. It's enough, though, to be the only witness to a short act in The Patch's nightlife. I'm left with the impression, though, that I've frequently felt before: that more happens during the shifts of darkness than any of us humans ever seem to realize.

Wednesday 4 February 2009

Satisfyingly, the harsh weather has continued and there are now some changes in wildfowl populations on The Patch. The widespread ice has raised the tufted duck population to fifty-five birds (from fifteen) and the pochard population to nine from two. Most of these are probably local birds fleeing iced-up ponds, but it is possible that some might have come over from the Continent, which isn't difficult for ducks because they are such powerful fliers. Most people don't realize, either, that ducks are among the fastest-flying groups of birds in the world. The trip from Holland, where many pochards spend the winter, is but an overnight hop – and male pochards, which most of these are, coincidentally have red eyes for their red-eye flights.

All but one of the arriving pochards is a male, and the sex ratio alone suggests that they are from the Continent. Male and female pochards make separate movements, a phenomenon known as differential migration. When their breeding season in Scandinavia, the Baltic states and Russia is over, male pochards move south first and quickly occupy suitable sites for wintering. By the time the females, who have been busy with chick-rearing, turn up, the nearest sites are full and they are forced to migrate further south, to Spain and beyond. Therefore, any influx of birds from the near Continent is likely to include a majority of males. If local birds were moving, one might expect a more even sex ratio.

Not that the pochards on The Lake are appearing remotely interested in my musings about their origin. They are, as pochards always seem to be, asleep. Every one of them has its head resting on its back and bobs around in the water like an anchored buoy, its webbed feet still working as a rudder despite the bird's apparently slumbering state. The pochards are probably loafing as much as sleeping, but they are definitely not feeding, not like the tufted ducks actively diving around them. Pochards are famously sleepy, and their behaviour can partly be explained by the fact that, on disturbed waters such as The Lake, they mainly feed at night. While the diet of tufted ducks veers towards mainly animal, pochards are primarily vegetarians, and the ease of finding plant material when it is dark probably explains the difference.

Meanwhile, the ducks are not the only visitors newly in. Something a great deal more unexpected has turned up on The Shire Field, and something a great deal more incongruous, too – a black swan. It has joined its close relatives the mute swans (these two are the only swan species to carry their newly hatched cygnets on their backs) feeding on the flood plain, and looks completely at home. The black swan looks like a mute swan that has been burnt to a cinder; its plumage is all black, but the body feathers have pale fringes, making the plumage look charred. The bill is pink, with a white tip. Only the main flight feathers, hidden under the tertial feathers, have escaped the scorching and are pure white.

I should have been happy with a new species of swan on The Patch, but I wasn't. A Bewick's swan, a rare Russian breeding bird which comes to southern England in small numbers each winter, would almost have been expected in these harsh conditions. A whooper swan from Iceland would have been a bonus, too, and made for a special day. But not a black swan, for goodness sake.

Let me explain. Black swans are from Australia and, in the history of bird migration studies, only one bird, a common tern, has ever been proven to fly between Britain and Australia. Terns are prodigious migrants, but wild black swans? A movement from state to state in Australia is a prodigious leap for them and the furthest they have ever wandered in the wild is to New Guinea, just a stone's throw across the Torres Strait. There is simply no chance that this bird is properly wild. It undoubtedly came from somebody's wildfowl collection.

The sheer number of exotic wildfowl that turn up in seemingly wild places in Britain is quite astonishing. Keeping ducks, geese and swans in captivity is obviously pretty popular, and it tarnishes the reputation of many a truly wild bird that turns up under its own steam. Our early February black swan, at least, is unequivocally of captive origin.

The former owners should know that a black swan is for life, not just for Christmas.

Friday 13 February 2009

Something stirred the birding runes today and produced an unexpectedly rich helping of good species. There was no obvious reason in weather or season for it, nor do I recall living my life with excessive virtuousness in the preceding days. Instead, it was a patch-watcher's gift.

The Patch certainly needed an immediate antidote to the black swan of the last trip, and it came today in the form of my first record here of Egyptian goose. You might wonder what the difference is between these two exotic wildfowl, one from Australia and one from Africa, and why one is the antidote to the other. The distinction is their current status in the UK. Black swans have no 'proper' legitimacy; if you like, they don't have the ornithological equivalent of a residence permit. Egyptian geese, on the other hand, have been living wild here since 1678 and have built up a very healthy and completely self-sustaining population in the natural environment. Their residence permit, namely official acceptance on to the British List, has been held since the 1970s. This means that, if you build up a list of birds that you have seen anywhere, then you can count Egyptian goose but not black swan – or at least, not until the Aussies start blackening our rivers and lakes.

None of this should matter at all, but we birders are quite conservative and routinely take the relevant committee's diktats to heart. Thus I find myself indifferent to the swans, but more than a little chuffed to have seen the Egyptian geese – which is pretty silly, if you think about it.

Egyptian geese are weird birds, a classic example of a species that looks as though it has been created from spare parts. The colour scheme, in particular, is bizarre, and the birds walk as if their legs are just a little bit too long for them, and their neck hasn't been attached properly. Their most distinctive feature is a dark brown patch around the eye, which makes them look as though they are wearing shades, and is very conspicuous against their whitish neck. The wings are stunningly colourful, with a bold white shoulder patch and a green iridescent trailing edge, completely out of keeping with the body's khaki colour scheme. The legs are long and bright red, and the birds sport a peculiar dark splodge in the middle of the breast, like a misplaced beauty spot.

The two visitors are treating The Patch as their own, which is another way of saying that they are courting shamelessly. Geese don't have much with which to display, so this involves a great deal of neck-stretching and swaying, and no doubt mutual admiration for the other's 'shades'. If they do decide to breed here, they will have to go house-hunting next to The River where the woods are; these curious birds usually nest in a large hole up in the treetops.

It so happens that they are being observed by a character that could easily put their future hopes and dreams in doubt – a fox. Indeed, the love-struck birds wander within a couple of metres of a sunbathing dog. However, the fox doesn't flinch and doesn't make the slightest attempt to catch them. It is either well fed, or has the same general thoughts in its head as the geese do. But it could have been a narrow squeak at best.

Oddly enough, another bird to show up today is the Egyptian goose's closest relative, the shelduck. One might be called a goose and one might be called a duck, but neither is either, strictly speaking. They share some characteristics with ducks (nesting in confined spaces) and some with geese (the male and female look alike), but most of their relatives live in South America. The shelducks are one of The Patch's more interesting breeding birds. Usually associated with the coast, shelducks are uncommon inland, but they like gravel extraction sites and probably use rabbit burrows within The Quarry for their nests. They have appeared today for the first time this year, which in itself is the result of a very curious quirk of migratory expedience. After breeding, all the adult shelducks quickly go on what can only be described as an extended holiday, leaving their well-grown chicks behind them in the care of a few young adults (Social Services, take note). Their destination is the northern coast of Germany, where there is an enormous system of shallow sea and mudflats, as far as the eye can see. This site is safe from ground predators, who shun the dangerous sands, and provides them with plenty of food – and if you're a shelduck, what more could you possibly ask for? While there, the adults moult their wing-feathers and have a brief flightless stage, which is the actual reason for massing at this one safe place. But, rather than returning quickly from this 'moult-migration', they remain on the Heligoland Bight for months and months, basically enjoying an extended shelduck knees-up: eating, socializing, more eating, preening, eating again. And who can blame them? By the late autumn some drift back to the wintering areas, but not all. And it seems perfectly possible that some simply stay put, until at last the spring – or in this case February – begins to prompt them to return. The impression is of a lifestyle of hedonistic abandon, which makes the shelduck the ornithological equivalent of a beach bum.

Friday 20 February 2009

Every patch birding trip begins before it begins. That is, it forms in the mind's eye, and has an identity long before the binoculars come out. For example, today is mid-February, and in the few minutes it takes to drive here from home, my mind will be imagining encounters with unusual species of gulls, or ducks, or finches. Patch-watching is different from normal birding, in that you need to have a reason to make the trip. Anybody travelling to Norfolk in October knows that they will be swamped with birds, and the trip will be special; they need no specific reason, or target, to persuade them out of bed. But at a patch something must compel you to get out on that specific day at that specific time. And that reason, invariably, must be an imaginary one.

Look at it another way. If patch-watchers knew exactly what they were going to see on a birding trip, they might not bother to go, especially if it was the same, by and large, as they encountered last time not long ago. Thus, they are attracted mainly by the possibility of seeing something different and special: something that, at first, is imaginary. The imagination, therefore, is one of the crucial driving forces in that peculiar allegiance formed between patch and watcher.

Today's imaginary bird happens to be an Iceland gull. Gosh, shivers go down my spine thinking about Iceland gulls. They are Arctic breeding birds and they look like them too, with very pale-grey plumage, completely white wing-tips and very pink legs; yet their appearance, for all its singular appropriateness, is not what causes the shivers. It is their scarcity combined with their origin that makes them exciting, together with a coaxing tendency to turn up on inland gravel pits just like mine. The thing is, imaginary though the Iceland gull might be at the moment, it is not a far-fetched fancy. I really might see an Iceland gull today, and that would be a rich delight because I have never seen one here before. It really might happen. In the same way, a young man might fantasize about catching the eye of a famous Hollywood actress, but his real excitement will come the day he gets a look from Debbie in Accounts. The real thrill comes when the imaginary blends with the possible.

So I rush to the edge of The Quarry fuelled by anticipation, and I am soon concentrating fervently on the gull flock that has parked itself, tantalizingly, not far away. Using a telescope, I am soon lost in a world somewhere between myself and the birds. It's a pleasantly warm February day, but the only thing that matters is through the lens.

One of the many positive features of gulls is that they stay still and you can check them through in detail. I work from left to right. Half an hour later, I have seen plenty of gulls, but not an Iceland gull, nor even a bird that might be an Iceland gull. Several more checks confirm the negative. I feel crushed. In fact, everything I have seen today is almost exactly the same as I saw last week. The same mix of gulls has gathered on The Quarry with the same cast-list of ducks and pretty much everything else. The only bright spark was an unusually high count of lapwings. They are delightful birds, but they aren't the birds I was hoping for.

Patch-watchers suffer hundreds of days like this. They are the bread and butter days when, had you known that you wouldn't see anything special, you wouldn't have bothered to go birding at all. They aren't the days when you are doing something useful, like counting the ducks for a national survey, or just doing a general count to compare what is seen from year to year. These bread and butter days are the days that you hope will bring a personal gift in the form of a something noteworthy.

I suppose these days are also valuable. These are the days, dispiriting though they are, that actually make the special days special when they come around. If you always saw something unusual when birding, it would raise your expectations to an unsustainable level and you would quickly become bored. The bread and butter days are also the trips when, bored by just the identity of a bird, you might actually stop and watch it and get to know it better. So they do have a value.

But the fact is: boring days don't feel valuable. And that's why, when it comes to the next time, you need your imagination.

Wednesday 25 February 2009

Today's imaginary bird was the Jack snipe, a small straw-coloured wading bird. I took a visit to The Patch in the evening with a view to finding this shy creature which, as far as this part of England is concerned, is as elusive as the local pumas that reportedly stalk the woods and farms nearby. Jack snipes like it damp, and today has been very damp. It is as if somebody had taken a giant sponge and squeezed it all over the countryside. Puddles are lying everywhere on the fields and farmland. The River is straining at its leash, ready to burst its banks. Every leaf of every bush and blade of grass is adorned with a queue of small droplets, which wait in turn to tumble to the ground.

Jack snipes need wellington boots and a sense of adventure. The best way to see them is to walk within a ditch or stream and flush them from the bank. This very proactive approach is necessary because Jack snipe don't fly away like normal birds. In contrast to the snipe, which is so nervous that you can imagine it flushing when you are still at home getting your boots on, the Jack snipe simply crouches down and hopes you walk past. It only moves when you are about a metre away, and sometimes not even then; incredibly, there are records of bird-watchers actually stepping on Jack snipes that have fatally decided that camouflage is the best policy. So on a damp February day, when nothing much else is about, a Jack snipe expedition is standard birding procedure. The stream on the edge of The Shire Field looks ripe habitat, although I muse that it might be safer to bring an aqualung than waterproof boots to cover this treacherous stretch of vegetation-clogged water.

As it happens, none of this is relevant, because if the local Jack snipes haven't been flushed, they've been squashed. A small band of lads on quad bikes have got to The Shire Field first, and are enjoying the challenge of the sodden field. I should point out that they are entitled to be there, but I am downhearted nonetheless. The noise has flushed everything from The Lake, and The Patch's usual sense of calm has been routed.

The quad bikers are a rarity in these parts, which is one thing that cannot be said about another disturbance factor on my

Patch and many others – dogs. This evening there are quite a number of them about, and at first sight there is nothing in the scene that one might object to: just a variety of people, each accompanied by a four-legged friend, everybody keeping fit. Among the various canine-human combinations, the majority take heed of the signs all around The Lake pleading for the bone-eating part of the family to be kept under control. However, at least two combinations are allowing their dog free rein, and the animals are understandably running around as nature directed them. One is actually splashing in the water, a good fifty metres away from its owner, who is proclaiming her moans about life down a mobile phone, evidently to a friend who is hard of hearing.

To me, this is an example of a curious casual disobedience, and it's hard to escape the conclusion that a routine, workaday disregard of signs is endemic, or becomes so, among a small but persistent proportion of dog-walkers. When The Quarry was not only shut to the public, but also represented a potential danger to anyone who might take a step into the deep excavations, I frequently saw dog-walkers simply flout the signs and wander with their doggies wherever they liked. Strangely, I never saw an ordinary walker do this, and it makes me think: is there something about walking the dog that produces a curious militancy among gentle folk? When a normal person would typically heed any sign that they could read, would the ownership of a dog make them more likely to start ignoring those same signs?

What happens at The Patch seems to suggest that it does.

MARCH

Wednesday 4 March 2009

It's a curiosity of birding generally that the most fleeting of glimpses can turn an ordinary excursion into an unforgettable one. Today I had such an incident, in which a day turned on a few seconds of distant acquaintanceship, and a moment opened a window into the extraordinary.

I had completed the most routine of inspections of The Patch, counting the gulls (eleven lesser black-backed gulls, quite good) and ducks (forty wigeon) as usual. The only memorable part of the trip up to the point of departure was the weather, which was fickle, with sunny patches interrupted by violent outbursts, including a ferocious hailstorm. These were merely the first rumblings of a weather clash that led to heavy snow the following day, but they were enough to make things decidedly unpleasant for all The Lake's occupants. Even the gulls, the largest versions of which have a distinctly macho appearance, so that you can imagine a herring gull continuously chewing gum, were struggling to cope with the increasing gusts of wind, grimly swimming with their heads into the wind and their wings tightly shut.

Yet amidst this turbulence I caught a glimpse of a small bird battling its way over the far side of The Lake, and was astonished to see that it was a sand martin. A sand martin is a slim, brown version of a swallow, and while swallows, with their swept-back wings and long tail streamers, give the impression of a certain power and determination, sand martins, by contrast, always look like weaklings. Even in calm conditions they look fluttering and feeble, holding their wings in close to their bodies as if they were embarrassed by their lack of finesse. On this particular day the sand martin looked no more in control of itself than a patch of spray from a wave, as it was whisked along by the wind. As a summer visitor, like the swallow, it was a harbinger of the coming spring. But spring was officially cancelled today. Within seconds it was blown out of sight, like an unwelcome heckler hustled away by a politician's minders.

It's true that the first sand martins usually turn up in Britain in March, but as everyone knows, there is March and March. In this most two-faced of months this individual was at least two, if not three weeks ahead of its peers, and it was the earliest arrival I had ever seen.

What induced this individual to leave the heat of West Africa for the negligible charms of England in very early March? In a word, power. For any species that is migrating north to breed in a temperate country such as ours, arrival time is very important. If any individual, in particular a male, can arrive on its breeding grounds earlier than the rest, it will find it has the pick of the best territories and, because possession is nine-tenths of the law, it will almost certainly keep what it finds. Holders of the best territories attract the best potential mates and enhance their opportunity to raise young successfully. We might hold a romantic view of early arrivals – the swallows bringing the promise of warmer weather and happier times – but the reality is all about being at the head of the queue.

The earliest arrivals in a population are invariably the older and more experienced birds. But they are also the risk-takers. Those that arrive during a cold snap of weather are playing with their lives. The arrival of migrants is a game of high stakes.

Unfortunately, today's bird is almost certainly a loser in that game. Within hours heavy snow was dumped all over the country and the temperatures dropped to lethal levels. There would not have been any flying insects to feed a needy sand martin.

It was strong. It was bold. But I'm sure I was the last person to see that sand martin alive.

Thursday 12 March 2009

Two birds were present in record-breaking numbers today. But apart from the coincidence of their numbers, these two characters have little in common. One is overlooked and underrated; the other is an icon.

On the large field next to The Farm was a large gathering of stock doves, numbering thirty-nine in all. Smart, pert, thundercloud-coloured pigeons, they all had their heads down busily in the newly growing clover, munching their early spring appetizer with the relish of customers at a smart restaurant. Occasionally one or two would fly up and there would be a flicker of soft grey, as if the wind had disturbed some ashes off a bonfire. It's hard to know where such large numbers come from; there were twice as many as I have ever counted before. One or two pairs nest in crevices around workings of The Quarry, but I can only assume the rest come from much further away, in the larger deciduous woodlands several kilometres from The Patch. Who knows, perhaps some come from one of the forests not far away? If so, each has commuted from its tree hole high in the canopy of tall, ancient woodlands – not far, but a different world from here.

There were plenty of people around The Lake today, but

nobody else noticed the stock doves, I'm sure – that is the way for this bird. It looks like a woodpigeon and so everybody writes it off as having no value or worth. Yet it is the less common and smarter version of the pigeon, with a song as delicate as a whisper and as easily missed. I promise you, it is a bird for the connoisseur.

The other species to beat its previous record would need no champion to plead its worth. The Shire Field mute swan herd (it's too big and important a bird to form 'flocks') has now reached the fifty mark. Numbers have been slowly building all year, and they are beginning to make an impressive sight, dotted across the fields by The River.

You might wonder: 'What are fifty swans doing crowded together in mid-March, when they should be on territory?' But the answer is that none of them will breed this year at all. They will mainly be youngsters (indeed, some still retain some brown feathers), although there are some whose productive days are behind them and are grazing out their existence. Swans don't start nesting until they are at least three years old, and until then they will remain in flocks like this among others of their own age. It is a good place to find a partner; on these lazy fields even today, the germ of a long-term relationship could be sprouting – affection and excitement for the future.

Great Birding Days

Thursday 21 March 2002

We took a dirt track, and it led us to one of those well-built wire fences that protect something significant, but have no signs or information. My wife and I were on a walk of serendipity, an afternoon to escape from the bubble of Carolyn's pregnancy, an outing on which to take deep breaths and follow our curiosity. To us, not much more than a kilometre away from our house but covering new ground (we had recently moved here), the fence was of course irresistible. It was a 'wonder what's behind it' fence – the kind that is supposed to repel, but actually attracts, drawing you closer and closer until you have pushed your nose against it.

To be truthful, there wasn't much behind it: only a large, deep pit with steep sides. At the bottom of the pit there were a couple of piles of gravel higher than the rest, and upon these rested a small gathering of bored-looking large gulls. They were the sort of group that remind me of teenagers, who look at you with utter indifference, but then shuffle away, one by one, as if they have been caught in the act of doing something wrong.

To almost anybody but a birdwatcher, the scene would have been a disappointment. But I *am* a birdwatcher. And all bird-watchers know a gravel pit when they see it, because throughout the country there are bird-filled lakes that started as pits. As I rested my hands on the barbed wire, I began to imagine the future; even then, on my very first visit to The Patch. This pit would soon be filled with water and over the coming months and years it would begin to attract birds. Where there was now gravel, there would soon be habitat. The pit was empty of everything but promise.

It was even more of a bonus to turn up at what was, in natural history terms, an important moment for The Patch itself. It was a potentially good birding site in the early stages of production. The scenes weren't yet complete, the characters hadn't been auditioned, and the script was only in the imagi-nation. I was in at the start, the first member of the audience. I was in the privileged position of being able to watch The Patch's potential become realized.

And although there wasn't much to see yet, the possibilities, even on this first visit, made me giddy with anticipation. There was already a skylark singing in an adjoining field, and on the top of one of the gravel sides a small flock of finches were processing dandelion and other weed seeds, standing in a line in studied concentration, as busy and preoccupied as miniature factory workers. Among their number were five goldfinches, twenty linnets and, quite unexpectedly, three lesser redpolls. These last, with their raspberry-coloured foreheads, black bibs and yellow bills, were evidently taking a spring break from their normal diet of birch seeds.

It was eight years before I saw another lesser redpoll at The Patch. But even on this first visit, the idea of watching for redpolls in eight years' time seemed entirely plausible. I had my Patch.

Monday 23 March 2009

To a patch-watcher, March is gull month. It's a month of tremendous turnover, with the mix of gull species being spewed out differently day after day. As a result, the gulls mark the passage of the seasons more reliably than the arrival of birds like swallows. Not only do gull movements start earlier than those of traditional summer migrants, but they are also more solid and less weather-dependent than the patchy arrivals of birds coming from far away. That's why it is possible to estimate the date from a register of gulls, while the first arrival of a swallow might be a freak, as was the appearance of the sand martin three weeks ago.

Up and down the country, then, patch-inclined birdwatchers count their gulls feverishly in March, revelling in those statistics that measure the arrival of spring. Gulls are great for birdwatchers – big, white, easy to see, and often very tame – and so they ought to be popular everywhere. Yet strangely, many wildlife enthusiasts, and even keen birdwatchers, have scant regard for them. At best they are ignored, at worst they are vehemently disliked.

In truth they have a serious image problem, almost as bad as that of pigeons, and it is utterly baffling. Yes, there are lots of them and they are pretty noisy, but they do remarkably little harm. Anyone would think they were like flying wolves, seemingly 'terrorizing' hapless people at seaside towns by flying down and mobbing them; indeed, in 2010 the Royal Mail suspended postal deliveries to a street in Devon because of a few dive-bombing gulls. For goodness' sake – what kind of lily-livered state have people reached? Yes, sometimes gulls in seaside towns will – perish the thought! – nick people's chips, and a few people have received pecks on the head. But come on, Britain, it should be a privilege to have such a close encounter with a wild animal. The average British motorist is more aggressive than any gull.

Other seasiders complain that gulls have the temerity to nest on people's roofs and – can you believe it? – make a lot of noise. Councils purse their collective lips and talk about culling them. But when you think of the seaside, what sound does it invoke? Yes, the wailing of seagulls, of course. When people live by the sea, they expect the sound of gulls to be part of the atmosphere. People get used to the sound of traffic and, near airports, to the sounds of planes. Why can't they just get used to gulls and stop bleating?

The fear and dislike of gulls is borne of the same ignorance and idiocy as a dislike of pigeons. Yes, gulls are noisy, but at least it's authentic, wild noise. Yes, they can be opportunistic, taking scraps off tourists – but isn't that another quirk of seaside living, which will make a good story to tell around the fireside? And as for nesting on roofs – well, why not? We make flat roofs, and gulls are completely entitled to set up territory on them, especially when cliff tops and beaches are becoming fewer in number because of us. A gull colony makes a good soap-opera. Stop complaining and get watching. Gulls are spunky characters and highly entertaining.

Anyway, the passage of gulls at The Patch is well under way, and the big news for today is that not a single common gull found its way onto today's log. The absence of common gulls marks the official end of winter. There were up to twenty-two common gulls present in January, then eight in February, and then a handful up until just one last week, the sixteenth of the month. There have never been any records from The Patch throughout the period from April to September; they disappear up to their breeding sites in Scotland and Scandinavia, and they don't come back here until the true winds of autumn breathe over The Lake.

Not that many people notice. Even among unheralded gulls, common gulls are overlooked and underappreciated. It's partly the name, a real turn-off. What could be more common than a common gull? Actually, they are not as common as the epithet implies, but they are still widely numerous. They are a little difficult to identify, but not a nightmare. The truth is that the grey on their backs is smart and intense and as typical in winter as the frost on the grass. I look forward to their return.

Meanwhile, today also brought a transformation in the numbers of lesser black-backed gulls. There is now a peak of forty-four individuals, suggesting that their migration is in full swing. On 12 March there were only thirteen lessers here, while back on the ninth there were ten, and on 13 February we had just four birds, less than a tenth of what are here today. (Numbers declined to twenty-five by the end of March.) It might seem odd to speak in terms of gull migration, but their journeys are just as much migrations as those of swallows and cuckoos, going back and forth, north in spring and south in autumn. Here at The Patch, lesser black-backs are extremely seasonal, appearing in large numbers only in March and April. The birds appearing now have almost certainly spent the winter on the Continent, or even as far south as North Africa, and are working their way northward to breed somewhere in the north of England. These birds around today are extremely smart, with their long, narrow wings and thundercloud-grey backs. It's exciting to see them in such numbers because, within a couple of weeks, hardly any will remain.

There is still another gull to mention. It is a special one, the Mediterranean gull. And if you can't bring yourself to accept that a gull could ever be described as special, you've never seen a Mediterranean gull in breeding plumage: it is as smart and smooth as a waiter in a top-class restaurant. The head is truly black (unlike a black-headed gull, which has a brown head – don't ask), except for a white crescent above each eye, while the wings are almost pure white, with just a thin black line along the leading edge of the outer wing. Furthermore, the bill is a deeper, more blood-red colour than the bill of any other gull. The result is one seriously good-looking bird.

These gulls are special for another reason, too. They were once very rare in Britain, breeding no nearer to here than the coast of the Black Sea, where they fed on insects during the summer. In the 1950s, however, a remarkable westward expansion occurred, first to Hungary and then to the seaboard of Europe, including France and Holland. The first pair to nest in Britain did so in 1968, and by 1979 the Mediterranean gull became a regular breeder, having never looked back from this point. It hasn't quite exploded in the style of the little egret, with a foothold of just over a hundred breeding pairs, but in any given winter there are about two thousand birds present in Britain, with perhaps most in the spring. At any rate, today The Patch is honoured to host a couple of these recent colonists, and it feels all the better for their good looks and pioneering spirit.

The sheer delight of seeing Mediterranean gulls and even lesser black-backed gulls is, I suppose, one of the marks of an enthusiast, and if you don't share a delight in gulls it cannot be inculcated in you. But every devotee starts somewhere, and for me it was a very routine epiphany. One evening I studied the introduction to a book called *Gulls – a Guide to Identification*, by the late and sorely missed patron saint of birding, Peter Grant. It explained the moult sequences and made gull identification seem possible. Gull identification – possible? I have been hooked ever since.

Monday 30 March 2009

What to do on a Monday lunchtime? Sit at the desk and continue working; read a magazine; go shopping perhaps. You can have a gossip with a friend and colleague. Or, of course, you can be bedazzled by the antics of spectacular birds on your patch.

Of course, I didn't know that this visit was going to be a treat; one cannot accurately predict any birding trip. But it was a balmy late March day, with warm sunshine, high cloud and a light wind, so the fresh air would have been enough.

Days such as this are good raptor days, which is just as well, because there was very little about on The Quarry or The Lake, just a few gulls and ducks. But the sky provided a good canvas for bird of prey action. Within a few minutes, one of The Patch's buzzards rose above the trees in Samuel's Wood and began its usual routine of wheeling upwards, its wings held in a shallow 'V'. Buzzards tend to wheel in narrow circles, as this bird did, as if they are trying to rise up a vertical chimney, and for a bird of their size, with long, broad wings, they make flying look surprisingly difficult. Whenever they flap, their wing-beats are stiff and shallow, and they seem neither dashing, in pursuit of prey, nor effortless in their mastery of the air. Their relative abundance is a mystery to me, because I have almost never seen a buzzard actually catch any prey – or at least, not difficult prey such as a flying bird or a running rabbit or vole. Yes, you can often see them gathered together in ploughed fields, where they simply trot about catching earthworms; and you often see them perched on fence posts or poles, presumably ready to pounce on something edible down below. But have you ever seen one swoop down from the sky and snatch fleeing prey with a dexterous turn of the talons? Neither have I. Buzzards must catch food, however, because there are lots of them about. Some definitely take carrion and road kills, but even these birds must have the ability to take live prey.

A glance at the tail of the buzzard showed that it bore a dark band near the tip, characteristic of an adult. It uttered a couple of wild-sounding mews in an uninterested attempt to sound territorial, and disappeared below the horizon.

It was quickly replaced by a male sparrowhawk, arriving from the west in the open skies, and working its way across The Quarry with its customary mixture of fast flaps and slightly unsteady glides. Halfway along it seemed to catch a fancy for the gentle conditions, so it broke its journey and began to soar upwards, showing off the orange colour of its breast, together with the typical sparrowhawk long tail and rather short, blunt-tipped wings. For once there wasn't a crow about to challenge its presence and mob it off the territory, so it simply kept on rising until it seemed to vaporize at great height under the sun.

It is curious to compare a birdwatcher's typical experience of these two species. If buzzards are in your area, you see them frequently and easily and they hardly ever seem to be hunting, let alone catching anything; sparrowhawks, by contrast, you come across much less often, but when you do they are often involved in a lightning strike at food, whether it be a group of birds at a bird-table, or perhaps a flock of larks or finches in a field. A flock of feeding birds will often ignore a buzzard flying over in plain sight, but the very suggestion of a sparrowhawk is enough to tip them into a panic, scattering in all directions, diving into cover and cowering down for a few minutes after-wards. Clearly, buzzards are food generalists that mainly take mammals and carrion and very few small birds, while sparrow-hawks are small bird specialists. But the different reactions they engender among the bird community are still remarkable.

Two species of birds of prey cannot be ignored, whatever patch you watch, but it turned out that the lunch break yet had some-thing extra special in store, something still more dangerous and charismatic. As soon as the sparrowhawk had melted away into the glare of the sun, a quite different character arrived, of similar size to the sparrowhawk, but with a shorter tail and sharply pointed wings: a peregrine. Where the sparrowhawk had looked strong without being powerful, this predator simply commanded the skies, sailing the breeze in speedy, muscular, macho style. The slightest twitch of its scimitar wings turned its body, and the slightest of twitch-flaps gave it that lavish acceleration that inspires such awe among those who admire birds of prey. With the sun upon it, it was easy to make out its dark, heraldic hood, barred white breast and lead-grey upperparts, while its thickset body, broad at shoulder and hips, made it look like a kestrel on steroids. The peregrine is possibly the world's most dangerous predator to other birds, but this bird was content to describe wide circles in the air, in sky-dancing, playful mood.

By many measures the peregrine is a cut above other bird predators. The most famous record that it holds is as the world's fastest flying bird, which also translates as the world's fastest self-powered animal of any kind. When dropping down from a great height onto prey, using flaps and then gravity – a manoeuvre known as a stoop – the peregrine certainly exceeds 160 kph and may well touch 290 kph at times; not surprisingly, when it strikes a bird such as a pigeon or duck at such a speed, it breaks the poor victim's neck. Furthermore, it is likely to be able to break the 160 kph barrier in level flight, too. But for me, impressive though its speed undoubtedly is, the most admirable thing about the peregrine is its domination of the world. It occurs on every continent and is one of the most widespread of all warm-blooded vertebrates. And incredibly, it has been recorded preying on almost a thousand species of birds, which is 10 per cent of all species on earth.

Having a peregrine on your patch is therefore akin, one might say, to a state visit. And on this sun-blessed day, as the peregrine circled, it was joined by another, doing exactly the same, almost lazy, soaring routine. Every so often the two birds would co-ordinate their circles so that they came close to touching. There was no aggression, and in view of the fact that one bird (the female) was noticeably larger than the other, it was evident that this was a pair indulging in a touch of courtship.

It was like enjoying lunch with the king and queen.

APRIL

Thursday 2 April 2009

It's been wet recently and umbrellas seem to be growing all around the banks of The Lake. They belong to a new species for The Patch, at least officially: the angler. I mentioned in the Introduction that one of the realities of watching a patch is that it is liable to change in ways over which the enthusiast has no control. Well, now The Lake has officially opened up to fishing. There is a spanking new Visitor Centre especially purpose-built for those who bring rods and nets, there are ramps for fishing and reeds have been planted to give the fish some protection.

For seven years I have been used to having this place to myself, or largely so. Up until now, it has always been possible to wander around for two hours or more and not see another human being. Now, however, this is surely going to change. The banks of The Lake will be forever planted with umbrellas.

As far as birding this particular body of water is concerned, the fishing is unmitigated bad news. I don't have anything against angling at all (militant dog-walkers – that disagreeable constituency – are another matter), but when a person goes to fish, they are usually there for a long time, and simply by being there they are going to keep birds away. Herons will be interrupted in their feeding, and will the moulting ducks that I used to see every autumn come back again? I very much doubt it.

But the Water Company own the site and they are entitled to use it. It will make them a great deal of money. At least they will soon fill up The Quarry with water and create a huge new reservoir, and they reassuringly insist that there won't be too much disturbance there: no fishing, no boats.

I spot Ian Hayward, the water bailiff, by the new Visitor Centre and we have a chat. For him, the change in The Lake's use is a personal gift. As a mad-keen angler himself, he is like the proverbial child in charge of a sweetshop. He can barely keep himself from smiling as he talks about the next few years. Indeed, it seems that even the slightest thought about fishing brings him into a sort of quiet ecstasy. He is quietly passionate and a formidable advert for the sport.

'We've introduced carp, pike, perch and bream, rudd, roach, dace and tench', he says, beaming. 'And other species will make their way in. I have already found gudgeon and stonefish, and there will be plenty more', he continues, with the air of a man who has just won the lottery.

His infectious enthusiasm always mollifies my reaction to the anglers' presence. Ian is one of those people who loves his fishing so much that, while he talks about it, it doesn't matter what he is actually saying: the message is there. The Patch is fortunate to have him.

Anglers often speak about their love for wildlife and they often boast about their knowledge, too. I could never doubt the former, but the latter is often exaggerated. Today I got chatting with a man who was enthusing about this new fishing spot, and we got on to the subject of the anglers' enemies.

'There are certainly mink here', he declared. 'Lots of them. They eat the fish. In fact, one sometimes comes out of the reeds there and takes maggots out of my hand.'

He says this with conviction. Personally, I thought that mink and brown rats might look different enough to tell apart.

Monday 20 April 2009

It's the height of the breeding season and everything has multiplied, is in the midst of multiplying or is about to multiply. For some species it is all three, a multiplicity of multiplications. Some of The Patch's robins, for example, will have dismissed one brood to independence already, are in the process of feeding their second and will do their damnedest to try for another in the salad days of summer.

I paid a brief visit to The Patch around lunchtime and witnessed three breeding cameos. All three species were special in a way: gadwalls, house martins and the pair of little ringed plovers.

Evidently, not all was well in the gadwall camp. These ducks were unsettled, both literally and emotionally. This was obvious because a group of five was flying in circles over The Quarry's pools, occasionally landing for a short time, only to take off again almost immediately. There was one female, and she was evidently being pursued by no fewer than four males. There is always an uneven sex ratio among breeding ducks, with males outnumbering females (the females are far more vulnerable at the nest), but in gadwalls the pair bond is usually pretty strong and should be properly sealed by now. But presumably not here: communal flights occur when unattached males reckon they have a chance with a female. On the water, if a crowd gathers around her, the female urgently incites her mate to get rid of the unwanted attention, but if he is unable to do this or has disappeared from the scene, the female has no option but to try to shake off her unwanted suitors. The brouhaha caused by the pursuit is meant to summon the male from hiding or to allow him to assert himself once again. Thus these flights of an anxiously quacking female and randy, freewheeling males are entertaining to watch, but are probably quite stressful for the couple at the centre of it all.

One of the mysteries of The Patch is where these unusual

ducks breed. Gadwalls regularly stay around through much of the summer, with the females disappearing in telltale fashion at about the time they should be incubating. It could even be somewhere on The Quarry itself.

While the gadwall pairings are in a state of flux, the house martins probably haven't got that far yet. It is still hardly past the middle of April, and these birds have only just arrived, so at first I am surprised to see them lining up beside a muddy pool on the edge of The Quarry, just a few metres away, picking up the soft substrate in their bills. The mud, of course, is their nest material, but could they have reached such a stage so early? And then I remember: this is probably a male work party. When male house martins arrive at their old colonies their first task is to undertake refurbishments on the structures they used last year. Then, when the talent arrives in a few days or weeks from now, they can sing from their completed nests to attract a mate. Most of these early arrivals will be experienced birds, and they have probably been using mud from The Quarry for a number of years. The colony, only a small one of a few pairs, is under the eaves of the main waterworks building.

Dirty, muddy pools are an attraction for house martins, but somehow the two things don't seem to fit. House martins are invariably immaculately turned out, with their glossy blue-black back and inner wing-coverts and even more stunningly clean snow-white tummies and throat. And mud pools are, well, muddy. Furthermore, if you ever watch house martins on the ground you will see that their legs are covered in tight-fitting white feathers, making them look as though they are wearing white leggings or cricket whites, and so it seems even more ridiculous that they would risk getting their feet wet. But then, on the other hand, maybe those white legs are the equivalent of those trendy wellington boots that wander over the mud at Glastonbury.

For house martins, as much as for any British bird, nest building is hard labour. Most of us are familiar with the structures they build, the half-cups adhering to the top of a vertical surface almost flush to the roof above, leaving just enough room to poke the head out. These structures may be made up from as many as 1,500 different pellets of mud, all painstakingly gathered from the edge of a puddle, transported in the bill and then eased into the correct position within the nest structure. The mud needs to be of exactly the right consistency, not too wet and not too hard, so the bird needs the right sorts of puddles to be available during nest building. I estimate that these birds are flying about 270 metres between their mud source and the colony site, so if they were building a nest from scratch (as some birds may need to later in the season), they could be required to take as many as 1,500 round trips of 540 metres, which amounts to a simply mind-boggling 810 kilometres of flight just to collect their mud pellets. And that's without counting a quite substantial number of feathers that will also be added to the structure.

There seems to be no such burden upon The Patch's star breeding bird, the little ringed plover. This lunchtime I was treated to a performance of its display-flight, all exuberance and style. The bird flew around in big circles over The Quarry, flipping its body from side to side and giving off its understated sequence of repeated, harsh 'cree-a' calls. Every so often it landed right in front of me, taking a short break, before taking off on its circuits once more. There was no sign of a female and it seems that nothing serious has yet got going for the birds. It's odd, really, because as mentioned earlier, little ringed plovers are very early migrants, yet they don't seem to get their breeding act together until late May, or even June.

Tuesday 21 April 2009

You simply don't expect to take an evening stroll on your local patch and find yourself embroiled in a life and death struggle, do you? But this evening, that is exactly what happened.

The mute swan herd that lives on The Shire Field and on the flood plain beyond has a pretty cosy existence. They have water, shelter, lots of grazing, and hardly any territorial swan neighbours with whom to dispute and spat. But lying between their feeding areas and The Lake, where they roost, is a large and imposing pylon helping to deliver high wires across the countryside. Over the years I have seen a number of big corpses beneath this thirty-metre-tall giant, leaving a sorry mess of feathers and a windfall for the scavengers. But I never expected to witness a clash myself.

However, this evening a small herd of swans took off and began their imperious, if short, commuting flight. Swans fly with such regal grace that when they do come to grief it can be almost comical, rather like seeing an immaculately presented ice-skater crash down with splayed feet at the end of a triple-axle. One swan among the flock must simply not have seen the wires, or tried to inch through the gap between the upper and lower set. Either way, its wing caught the edge of a wire, all its momentum dissipated and it plunged down towards the ground.

It did not, however, hit the flat ground, but instead appeared to crash into the very deepest part of The Thicket. To be honest, the fall looked pretty bad. When they hit wires, swans usually break a wing or two. This swan had first hit wires, and then clattered into some quite unforgiving bushes.

What to do? I was in a dilemma at first. The initial option was to carry on watching and counting the birds on The Lake as if nothing had happened. This line of least resistance would spare me the agony of finding a bloody corpse, but could potentially also sentence the swan to a lingering, helpless death from starvation or from its injuries. Furthermore, with so many people about on this mild April evening, the official site undertakers, the local foxes, would not be along this way for a while to put an end to the suffering.

Of course, there was only one reasonable thing to do, and that was to see what had actually happened, so I wandered over to the crash site and peered into the vegetation. The mute swan is one of Britain's largest birds; it can weigh 15 kilograms and it is pure white. But a swan in a thicket turned out to be a needle in a haystack. It was a good ten minutes of scrabbling about in serious, prickly undergrowth before I found myself at last face to face with the bird, and by then, I estimated, we were both in equal need of hospital treatment.

The bird, it transpired, had survived the fall, for up close I could see that its eyes were open and, as I approached, the swan made a few cursory wriggles. It had ended up a metre or so above the ground, completely entangled in a small elder surrounded by hawthorns. One of its wings was caught on a branch, holding it open, while the other wing was held half-open at the same height. The swan was so stuck that it could have been a fly in a spider's web.

It was at this moment that I was forced to acknowledge that my ability to help the swan was not very much greater than the bird's itself. The sheer density of vegetation meant that I was almost pinned to the ground and could barely stand up. I had also foolishly failed to visit The Patch armed with all the equipment needed for a swan rescue. I had failed to bring gloves to protect me from bird, brambles and thorns; I had failed to bring a tarpaulin bag or some such that could be used to carry the swan if I could prise it from its predicament. I had brought a telescope on a tripod but, aside from poking the unfortunate bird, it seemed unlikely that this would help much. Most carelessly of all, I had not brought a mobile phone to give a call to the professional Swan Rescuers. Since the light was fading and the situation was dire, at least for the swan, I decided to throw caution to the wind and try to rescue the swan myself.

As you know, however, swans are not well known for their passive nature. There are swans in Oxford that routinely attack rowers, to such an extent indeed that assailants have been the subject of council meetings and hysterical press. There are swans everywhere that hiss fearsomely at anyone who passes.

There are also swans that have been known to menace cyclists, too – so they are not all bad. However, anybody who knows the temperament of mute swans would be a fool not to hesitate at the prospect of touching them, let alone trying to extricate them from a metre up an elder bush.

It was, therefore, hard to tell who was the more nervous as I gradually inched my way towards the swan. Interestingly, though, the bird hardly reacted at first. It was pinned tightly into its prison of branches, so it wasn't kicking about and struggling, but to my surprise it didn't even summon a hiss as I edged towards it clumsily and noisily. Perhaps young swans – for this was probably a bird under three years old as a member of its non-breeding flock – just don't hiss. Or perhaps this bird was so weak and traumatized that it didn't have the resolve to express displeasure.

My first fear was that the swan's wing, or even both wings, might be broken. My second fear was that there would be a nasty gash somewhere and lots of blood. Indeed both scenarios were likely. Call me squeamish if you like, but the idea of being covered by any animal's blood really doesn't appeal much, which suggests that I would have made a pretty poor Cro-Magnon. And I didn't like the idea of returning home looking more like a pathologist (or should that be a psychopath?) than a birdwatcher, to the inevitable alarm of my wife. But in fact, from one side at least, there was no hint of blood. All those feathers – and a swan, famously, has 25,000 of them – had obviously kept it from the barbs and spikes.

My second fear was allayed when the swan suddenly decided to make a run, or at least a flap, for it. Clearly terror had given it an adrenalin boost, and it managed to wriggle so hard that it dislodged itself after all. Ten minutes had passed since it had made contact with the power lines, and now this swan finally got down to earth. Extraordinarily, both wings were neatly folded to its sides, instead of hanging limply down, and it became obvious that it had had a miraculous escape.

Its redemption, however, was not yet complete. The swan was healthy and could walk and presumably fly, but it was still completely trapped. It was cowering under the thick undergrowth, and its way to the safety of The Lake was barred by a barbed wire fence; it was one of those really unpleasant, antisocial fences, too, which was no more than a metre tall but had the barbed stuff right at the top, ready for some misplaced genitals. The bushes grew right up to the edge, leaving very little room to climb through: a member of The Patch's fairy population might have found it a squeeze. The swan could no more take off and fly over this fence than a jumbo jet could manoeuvre from a helipad.

Thus the rescue was about to become personal; there was nothing for it other than to pick up the swan and lift it over the fence. It was at this moment that the entire human population, who had been swarming around The Lake a few minutes before on a hundred evening strolls, simply melted away, leaving the place deserted, when a couple of extra hands might have been helpful. And where is an angler on that single, once-in-a-life-time moment when you might actually need one? Having come this far, the swan and I needed to see the end of the affair.

The truth is that any spectators would have found the next little act in the drama hilarious. That is because the swan was no longer stunned and had come to its senses, understandably concluding that an impending embrace from human hands was not to its taste. It began to waddle up and down the fence, in the opposite direction from my waddle, so that several times I made a grab and ended with nothing but dirt in my face. My heart was pounding, and I was beginning to panic in case the swan now managed to injure or even kill itself, which would have been a sorry end indeed. However, if the truth be told, a fall from a power line does not lead to a swan feeling at its razor-sharp best, and on my third or fourth attempt I finally managed to get a decent hold on the beast.

I have never read a swan-handler's manual, but common

sense would dictate that leaving the neck free when you are carrying one of these birds is possibly not best practice. I fully expected to be pecked, or at least struck by the swan's bill. But remarkably, once embraced, the swan once again went into its shell, and didn't even protest as I edged it up towards those dangerous wires. What impeded our progress, however, was the swan's extraordinary weight. I knew swans were heavy, but being aware that a swan can weigh 15 kilograms and actually lifting that bulk are two different things. Forcing the swan over the fence and away would be an athletic feat equivalent to tossing a caber at the Highland Games. By now, however, both of us had been injected with a dose of steel, and with a heave and a flap we managed to keep the swan's body and feet away from the dreaded wires. The white beauty flopped with a crash on to the path, steadied itself and ran-flapped its way towards the shore of The Lake. Once there it gave itself a good shake and floated regally in the direction of its bemused colleagues.

It was only then, of course, that a small party of evening strollers hove into view. They gave me a sideways glance as I lurked behind the fence, face, trousers and fleece caked in mud, tripod leaning crazily against the barbed wire, and with a few white ashes from the swan's explosive escape still blowing around my head.

'Evening', they said cautiously.

'I've just rescued a swan', I said.

They didn't reply. The swan just floated around with its colleagues without ceremony. Order returned to The Patch.

Tuesday 28 April 2009

Bird-wise, summer arrived today, with the appearance of the first swifts over The Lake. Forget about swallows making a summer; they never did. In fact, Shakespeare misquoted Aristotle, who actually wrote that 'One swallow doesn't make a spring.' How right he was. The first arrival of a swallow is not the arrival of spring; it's when swallows arrive in bulk that you can finally declare the fair season open. And as for the summer, that can only be marked when the swifts arrive in bulk, not the swallows.

Do sixty swifts sound like enough bulk? That is the number that passed through today. As a first appearance it was quite impressive, the birds taking over the lowest airspace as they sought insects hatching out over the water. With a front going through, and with the skies grey and forbidding, The Lake was the only decent place to catch food, and they were joined by sand martins, house martins and swallows.

Every year I forget how mightily impressive swifts are. In fact, if you take the aerial birds of Britain, the weakest and weediest flier arrives first (the sand martin, in March and April) and the strongest and fastest arrives last (the swift, in late April and early May), which would seem to be the wrong way round. But no matter; after watching the swallows and martins pass by in dribs and drabs over the last few weeks, today it feels as though the professionals have taken over. Swifts are like Formula 1, swallows maybe like Formula Ford and, frankly, sand martins are like go-karts in comparison. The swifts simply look big and powerful. Their wings are longer than the others, more streamlined, and are needle-sharp at the tip; when they shoot past at head height you will feel as though they are slicing through the air. Their manoeuvrability is truly astonishing, and they have an impressive turn of speed.

Laughably, during the morning one of the black-headed gulls on site evidently decided that it might be productive to try to catch swifts. This individual was one of several first-summer birds that were fielding mayflies rising from the water with dexterous turns in mid-air and dips down to the water surface. Its success was quite obviously going to its head, because every time a swift came within range, it made a lunge and attempted to tail-gate one of these athletes of the air. Whether it was being predatory rather than just practising its flying skills on a fast object I do not know, but taking the swifts' speed and momentum into account, the gull might just as well have tried to intercept a speeding express train.

Swifts don't breed on The Patch, which is hardly surprising because there aren't any tall buildings on site of the sort they could use. But these birds are still a mainstay of summer over The Lake. There are always some around between May and August, either taking advantage of the low-flying insects, as today, or simply passing over. They are here so often on their non-breeding grounds that it gives cause to wonder what swifts do all day. I mean, how often does one see them doing anything except for just flying about? They seem to have an extraordinarily leisurely, peripatetic lifestyle, largely free from any responsibilities.

Although for many swifts this is simply an impression born of the birds' ease in a medium we don't understand, for others it happens to be true. Swifts don't breed until they are at least two years old, but that doesn't stop the first-summer birds (youngsters hatched last year that are living their first summer of life) from coming north in the late spring, along with the adults, and plying British skies for the wind-borne insect life. These birds really can come and go where they want to. Although they ostensibly associate with a colony and observe the trials and stresses of pairing up and breeding, the young swifts are essentially that: observers. They watch and they learn, and for much of the summer their time is their own; you could say that they are revelling in a gap year. These are the swifts that you most readily see rising high up into the sky on hot summer evenings, circling into the darkening evening until they are only detectable by their far-off screams. The adults usually roost in the nest, but these youngsters keep airborne and skittish, living on snatches of sleep, carefree like students everywhere.

And remarkably, these swifts come 5,000 kilometres to Britain from Africa, and not for a single moment do they touch down here. That is a necessity only for birds with territories and nests. But for now, these youngsters have no attachments, not even to the land.

Thursday 30 April 2009

It doesn't matter how many times one sees certain types of bird behaviour, the appeal just never seems to wear off. Take the water display of the great crested grebe, for instance. It is one of the most graceful and classy pieces of bird courtship it is possible to see in Britain, or indeed anywhere else. You cannot watch it enough times. Honestly, if it was ballet, you would pay to see it.

The Lake, perhaps surprisingly given its excellent roll-call of fish, is not an especially good place for great crested grebes, and so its waters are normally sadly bereft of surface dancing. Currently there is nowhere for a grebe to put its floating nest, so it is perhaps unreasonable to expect to see behaviour closely caught up with maintaining the pair-bond on what is a non-breeding water. Today, however, something changed; two of the six great crested grebes that remained on The Patch were clearly in the mood for a 'what the hell' session of alfresco performing. And as ever, their act was spellbinding.

There's definitely an element of ballroom drama about the great crested grebe's water courtship, not least because the performers are so elaborately togged up for the occasion. This is especially so about the head, where the birds sport magnificent chestnut and black cheek plumes, or 'tippets', and two black fan-like head-plumes which erect in display. The tippets expand to give the birds an almost cobra-headed appearance, set off by the black crest, pink bill and brilliant red eyes. Quite what it must be like to see a great crested grebe eye-to-eye in mid-display I do not know, but it is hardly surprising that the zenith of most routines occurs when the birds are meeting each other face-to-face. In a sense, the grebes are splashed with extravagant make-up, as well as wearing their best plumage finery.

Great crested grebe ceremonies are elaborate affairs, with a number of completely different routines with different meanings. One can never catch all of the acts in this play at a single sitting, since some are confined to short periods of the season and different stages in the grebes' pairing life. However, there will usually be something going on at any one time during the spring and, with luck, it is possible to catch some pretty sensational moves.

So it was on this particular trip to The Patch, although I would have to say it was a gift. The idea of the visit was to look for some migrant birds, and I certainly wasn't expecting to be sidetracked by the normally lethargic crew of teenage grebes that customarily summer on The Lake. I was aware of them being there, but did not take the slightest notice of them until I heard, from their usual corner, a very characteristic braying that typically emanates from great crested grebes when they are aroused. I looked over and was delighted to see two individuals facing up to each other, necks erect and tippets fully extended so that they formed a ruff behind the cheeks. They were already indulging in a display known as head-shaking. Perhaps there was something in the air.

Head-shaking is the most frequent ritual among great crested grebes, and is the one that is easiest to see. In its basic form, the two birds simply face each other and shake their heads (an interesting reversal of human customs, because the shake of the head here very obviously means 'yes'). They don't sway together in time, nor do they try to mirror one another with the shaking, but in any head-shaking ceremony worth its salt the birds will break off from the full-frontal head-waggling to dip their heads down and preen the feathers on their back. And although this might seem like a turn-off, as if a human were to break out of a serious snog in order to check their shoelaces, it is actually part of the display. It isn't a real preen, but a quick, sensuous flick of the back feathers, presumably as telling as a woman feeling through the back of her hair. Known as habit-preening, it helps to accentuate the overall effect of the display. Here on the placid waters, my grebes were putting on a good show.

Interestingly, as in all grebe ceremonies, it was not possible to tell the sexes apart during this ceremony, at least not by what either bird was doing. Grebe rituals are interchangeable, in that either sex can swap roles and each can lead the dance, with the other following. Thus, one grebe and then the other would nod down to habit-preen while the other shook its head. And despite the fact that one individual was noticeably larger than the other, both birds were essentially doing the same things.

It is perfectly natural for head-shaking in great crested grebes to be the totality of the day's statement of togetherness, with the display quickly petering out into nothing as the birds resume their daily activities, even falling unromantically asleep. However, I was thrilled on this occasion to see both birds submerge immediately after they had swum apart. This was a good sign. Diving is the first stage in the celebrated weed dance, the display that every birdwatcher wants to see, and indeed must see. The moment they disappeared under the water, I fervently hoped that, when they came back to the surface, each would be holding a lump of weed in its bill.

Sure enough, this is what they did, and were thus armed for a much more intense and physical display of affection. If you've never seen a weed dance (many books on birds have pictures of it), you must first imagine two human characters catching each other's eye across a gap – perhaps a street or a park, for instance. Now you must imagine that they adore each other, and their instant reaction is to run forwards into each other's arms, in Cathy and Heathcliff style, until they fervently embrace and spin around in a shameless show of lovers' ecstasy. Once you have imagined this, and calmed down a little, you must assume that something similar is going to happen with the grebes. Glancing across the gap of water to see weed in the mate's bill, the birds indeed swim rapidly towards each other, closer and closer, until they look set for a head-on collision. They then rear up upon their feet, paddling furiously to keep their bodies upright, and for a moment hold a position breast-to-breast. This is hard enough for a grebe, but the birds also waggle their heads from side to side in the same way as they do when head-shaking, except that they both, of course, are carrying weed in their bills. It so happens that the dangling weed accentuates the head-shaking, and no doubt the stimulus, as it has a gravitational life of its own and sometimes scatters drops of water as it is waggled violently from side to side. For a few seconds the grebes keep this so-called penguin display going, until such time as they are compelled to sink back down to the water, whereupon they may well resume conventional head-shakes. After such exertion, it will be some time before they are ready again for such an energetic routine.

So far as I am aware, this weed dance by the great crested grebes constitutes a first for The Patch. It's every bit as exciting as a traditional 'first', the name birders give to an encounter with a new species, and it is indubitably more significant. Somewhere, perhaps beside some overhanging vegetation shading one of The River's quiet stretches, these great crested grebes will find a nest site after all. And then perhaps they will breed. The weed dance is suggestive of a lot more than a lazy summer slumbering with their necks rested upon their feathered backs.

MAY

Great Birding Days

Tuesday 1 May 2007

The best patch-watchers have certain things in common. They are skilled birders, certainly. They are obsessive, invariably. And they are able to get up at the crack of dawn every morning – unfortunately.

I'm sure that I simply don't have the DNA to be a consistent early riser. Either that or I'm just lazy and not committed enough. Either way, despite being an avid birder, my successful attempts to get to The Patch at dawn, or at least before the first dog-walkers have got out, don't add up to much over the course of a year. And that is unfortunate because, sadly for all of us who are owls by temperament, it really is the best time to look for birds.

Mayday in 2007 stands out for me, though, because not only did I get to The Patch at first light for once, but it also proved to be a dawn excursion that paid handsome dividends. Regrettably, on many occasions when I have stumbled reluctantly out of bed, it hasn't proven to be any better for birds at The Patch than if I had started at a reasonable hour. That is annoying but it proves

the point: the best patch-watchers get out there at dawn repeat-
edly. All the time – day after day after day.

But on 1 May I joined the ranks of proper patch-watchers
and was out before sunrise. This break in character did have a
purpose. The previous few days the various bird information
services had been buzzing with news of inland waders. It
seemed that there had been a window of favourable weather
conditions and these great travellers were pouring all over
Britain and delighting patch-watchers everywhere. Many of
them were making landfall, not only in the places on the coast
where one usually expects to find them, but on less traditionally favoured sites, such as inland gravel pits – inland gravel pits
such as The Quarry. Would one turn up here?

There is something special about getting caught up in a
national event, be it The Coronation, Live Aid, the World
Cup...or maybe an Exceptional Inland Movement of Bar-
Tailed Godwits and Whimbrels. And sure enough, on this
gilded day, a quick scan of the scope onto the most distant
flooded pit revealed a bar-tailed godwit, a single bird on its
journey between West Africa and the Arctic regions of Russia.
With its presence The Patch had caught the trend; today my
humble Patch was part of the national picture. It was the equivalent of a small village receiving a visit from the Queen.

The bar-tailed godwit is a special migrant. In the last few years
scientists in the Pacific have radio-tracked some individuals
breeding in Alaska and discovered that, once they have finished
breeding and fuelling, they migrate south to New Zealand to
spend the winter. It's a long way - and they make the journey in
a single flight. It goes on for seven days and nights and, when
the travellers finally touch down in Kiwi land, they have covered
over 10,000 kilometres – without stopping! They make the
journey using nothing more for fuel than the fat deposits they
have built up from their diet of worms and crustaceans.

And this bar-tailed godwit was as stir-crazy as might be
expected of a hyper-fit, well-fuelled world traveller. It treated

The Patch as just another departure lounge and, within a few minutes of showing itself, took off to the north and flew over the causeway between The Quarry and The Lake. It probably touched down next on the shores of the Waddensee in Holland, where godwits traditionally feed hard and flex their muscles before the final leg to the Arctic.

The godwit was off by 6.45 a.m., just as dozens of exciting birds undoubtedly are in the course of the year. The conclusion: patch-watching is for early birds.

Saturday 2 May 2009

As if it needed to be said yet again, one of the great joys of watching birds is that the scene is ever-changing. It is genuinely true that no day is exactly like another, because most birds are travelling constantly – so any patch of ground is similar to a human transport hub, where the make-up of people is different every day. The analogy is very apt, actually, because at a human transport hub some people make the same journey every day, some people use the hub seasonally, some use it once in their lifetime – and some actually work there, so aren't travelling at all. Just the same happens with the bird characters at any patch, anywhere.

A bonus of receiving visitors is that they bring the flavour of their homeland with them. At a train or air terminus one will hear different accents and foreign languages and experience moments of vicarious transportation. At a local patch the bird visitors can be equally evocative. A noisy, bellowing herring gull brings a taste of the sea, for example, and a passing redstart transports the hearer to the rich oakwoods of central Wales. And it so happens that, as of today, my Patch in southern England has been transformed into a bog in northern Scotland, or perhaps a pool in the taiga of Scandinavia. A redshank, a dunlin and eight whimbrels are all sharing the muddy sides of a pool in

The Quarry. If they all actually have 'homelands', it is surely where they choose to breed, and this connection makes them representatives of such places far away. If they can all fit together into the field of view of a telescope, with no southern softies nearby, then it is easy to imagine that, just out of eye-shot, is a wild, treacherous bog, peppered with white heads of cotton-grass, stretching in every direction. Such a fantasy is a harmless treat for a birder bound by allegiance to a patch. And indeed, the treat of watching such travellers locally can exceed the reality of seeing the same birds on those distant breeding sites, where they are expected to be seen, and aren't a birding bonus.

The way in which birds connect distant sites by their migration extends well beyond mere imagination. Take the case of these whimbrels, curlew-like migrants that have a bold dark stripe over the eye, here languidly prodding their kinked bills into the shallows for water snails and insect larvae. These individuals will almost certainly have wintered on the Banc d'Arguin, in Mauretania, some 3,000 kilometres away, where they wile away the days foraging over mud-banks and beds of eel-grass. They take this and that, but in early spring their diet becomes more and more dominated by fiddler crabs, which are highly nutritious but hitherto have been reticent about putting their heads above the tropical mudflats. However, the siren call of reproduction is too strong to resist for the crustaceans, and the male crabs cavort at the entrance to their burrows to attract mates, and even form 'herds' in the water. Out of their comfort zone, randy and distracted, the crabs are easier to catch at this time and the whimbrels ruthlessly harvest them and put on weight. But the most elegant connection is in the timing. It so happens that the activity of the crabs is related to the tide (they are most active at low water) and the time of day (they aren't very active late at night). Both of these are connected to the lunar cycle. And this means that the earlier the increased breeding activity of the crabs coincides with the new moon, the earlier the whimbrels can fatten up and begin their migration. So, the date of the whimbrels' appearance here in southern England is directly related to the life-cycle of a tropical fiddler crab.

Thus, with a little imagination, the flock of stripy waders brings an African flavour to a chilly May afternoon.

Thursday 14 May 2009

On today's agenda is one of the most enjoyable jobs of the ornithological season: the census of breeding birds. Now that the summer visitors have arrived and have joined the residents in passionately holding territory, I need to do a circuit around the whole of The Patch to check out what is singing, count everything and to see whether any birds are showing other breeding signs, such as nest-building or even carrying food for their young.

This is the sort of undertaking that feels like more than just birdwatching. It's a contribution to the overall knowledge of bird populations, a form of citizen science. In normal circumstances, when we go birding we are doing it for ourselves and it has little impact elsewhere. When we count breeding birds over a period of time, however, we are constructing a piece of a jigsaw which, when scientists put it together, will reveal the picture of how our common breeding species are doing. It feels like very grown-up birding.

The fact that little ringed plovers breed at The Patch is very significant, of course, and they are by far our rarest breeding bird. But there is something even more satisfying about finding out that The Patch has eight pairs of blue tits compared to six last year, or that the pair of grey wagtails on The River near The Weir has successfully brought four youngsters into the world this season. Again, it is the intimate nitty-gritty that brings the patch-watcher back again and again to bean-count the common birds.

Anyway, enough of the bird census plug. It's not really much of a morning for doing anything today, grey and a little blustery. I certainly don't feel like singing, and to be honest, you might reasonably expect that any self-respecting bird would be hunkered down in the nearest shelter, silently playing Scrabble, or whatever birds do in their spare time. But as soon as I enter The Patch's hallowed ground, there are voices yelling loud enough to be heard above the gusts of wind. The truth is they cannot help themselves. May is the glorious month when a person can stay out for all the hours of light, and not once hear the bird singers fall silent, not even for a moment: not in the midday lull, not in the afternoon, not even at coffee-time. One bird or another carries on regardless, so that the soundtrack of spring is even more persistent than the tuneless garbage that the department stores inflict on Christmas shoppers. And even when it is dark, some of these birds – sedge warblers and robins, for instance – just keep going, singing on and on, as if sunset never happened, too distracted to let details such as the darkness get to them. The owls, proper birds of the night, have sensitive ears and at times this nocturnal racket must do their heads in.

My first port of call is Emily's Wood, where I know I am guaranteed to pick out something interesting. And indeed, it is full of voices, all competing for broadcasting space. Most of them are spirited to the point of manic, like the wild clamour on a bidding floor, but it's a whisperer that turns my head. The treecreeper has a voice as delicate as a sigh, and its high-pitched, falling phrase is the aural equivalent of a leaf making a gentle descent to the ground, only to be hitched up by an updraft before finally settling to its resting place. Song in May can only come from a territorial bird, and this is the first concrete proof that I have of a treecreeper breeding on-site.

There are two chaffinches singing from Emily's Wood, one on either side of the path, and in a nutshell their performance provides a pithy commentary on the role of singing in a bird's life. For a start, it is obvious that both singers are males and indeed, for the vast majority of British songbirds, that is the rule: the rising skylark, the dawn chorus, the blackbird on the roof – all of them males. Female birds make short, perfunctory statements in order to contact their mate or call to the young, but they don't normally make those complex and often tuneful utterances of the males that we describe as song. A bird chorus is male and testosterone-fuelled, despite its shrillness.

Second, you only have to watch the chaffinches to sense their motivations and perhaps be challenged in your own perceptions of why they are singing. To the human ear, birdsong is a glorious wild gift, a ministry to the soul, a figurative warm flannel to the face. It's one of those true universal delights that, while it is available to everybody, still feels intensely personal to the listener, as if it were a concert with an audience of one. It takes a hard heart indeed – the sort of heart that might think of suing a farmer for allowing their cockerels to crow – not to feel alive and refreshed under a torrent of birdsong. Yet the impression it gives to people is remarkably different from the impression it gives to other birds. To another bird a song is not relaxing to listen to, quite the reverse. To a female bird it might be an enticement; but to another male it is a challenge. Male birds probably view each other's songs with the same mixture of annoyance and bemusement that we reserve for the latest execrable commercial for car insurance.

Song is advertising. Before each chaffinch sings, it lifts up its head, as if about to shout an announcement to a crowd, and then delivers a cheerful, accelerating phrase with considerable gusto and verve. The song ends with the sort of flourish that really should earn a burst of applause from listeners. But it is just the usual patter, salesman-speak, a declaration of a slogan which says: 'It's me.' May's day-long chorus, and the dawn chorus of each spring day, could be compared to some kind of trade fair: all the stalls are close together and the owners of each are advertising themselves noisily. Some of the stalls are advertising the same thing (they are the same species), but there are many products on offer (different species). And while the advertisers selling the same product take notice of each other, by and large different sellers ignore their neighbours.

At risk of taking this metaphor too far, if you do ever visit a trade fair, you will sense palpable tension between those sellers marketing the same products, and in the same way, here at The Patch, there is similarly tension in the air. It's obvious because, as soon as one of the chaffinches here in Emily's Wood finishes a song-phrase, the other is compelled to respond immediately; indeed, it might start its phrase before the rival's has ended, as if stepping on its ankles. As a result the wood resounds to a magnificent duet. And this is where, if you listen carefully, you can begin to appreciate that the birds aren't singing for pleasure. It is clear that they are compelled to sing out of rivalry.

What's at stake for the singing bird? Its future as a breeding individual is at stake. A bird cannot begin to breed unless it has acquired a territory to call its own, a small parcel of habitat that is private. The song, uninhibited, is therefore a bird's slogan of rights-holding. It has earned the right to keep territory, and the song is intended to discourage other males from intruding, although they sometimes do and a fight will determine the outcome of the challenge. Normally, however, aggressive though the singing is, it actually prevents conflict and spaces the territory-holders out. Any male bird will be able to hear that a fragment of habitat is occupied, and will tend to avoid it.

As I listen to the continuous chatter from Emily's Wood, from the rattling chaffinches to the metronomic, repetitive notes of the chiffchaffs singing their name, it is hard to imagine that these singers are being challenging, let alone aggressive. It's true that they come across as spirited and joyful, and I can identify with every human being who has been drenched in this glorious stream of natural euphony and would swear that it was nature's caressing anthem of joy. Yet it is actually a remarkably disharmonious harmony.

But enough of this musing, and back to the numbers. Emily's Wood, it turns out, has much the same bird population as last year, with three singing wrens, a robin, one blue tit, two singing blackcaps and, on both its edges, trilling greenfinches, to name a few. The long-tailed tits are present and using the same thorny hedge by The River for their nest as last year, while a pair of mistle thrushes appears to have used one of the tall trees for their early brood. These large thrushes often nest very early in the year, and some scientists have speculated that they do this because predators have not yet tuned in before April to the prospect of finding eggs or fledglings.

For anybody carrying out a census, annual declines or boosts in a place soon become obvious and feel personal. They shouldn't really: most bird populations are cyclical, with natural peaks and troughs, so if there are, for example, more or fewer tits on site than a previous year, then it is no cause for joy or alarm, as checks and balances will inevitably follow. However, it is always a relief to make acquaintance with The Patch's more vulnerable birds, those undergoing national declines or those with locally tender populations. For example, there is but a single singing sedge warbler on The Patch, on the edge of The Marsh, and the spring wouldn't feel complete without hearing its usual, long-winded tirade of scratching and swearing notes. Similarly, I am also delighted to hear a cuckoo today, as I have in previous years, although they don't ever seem to stay. Cuckoos are in serious trouble in southern Britain, with an 80 per cent reduction in numbers in the last twenty years. Although the bird singing next to The River could be a migrant passing through, it is possible that there is a quiet female lurking nearby with designs on the small birds. If that is so, it would be really welcome...except by the reed warblers, of course.

I don't often reflect on what The Patch was like before it was transformed by The Lake and The Quarry, but there's little doubt that, if it was a standard parcel of typical English farmland twenty or thirty years ago, it would have resounded to the sonorous calls of cuckoos all through the spring. With The River here and its small fragments of reed-bed and willow scrub, the habitat would have been right. This is a bird that is all but lost locally. Nobody seems to know precisely why, although it might have something to do with declines in the numbers of hairy caterpillars available, or perhaps to do with wintering conditions in Africa, so it could be a local problem, or it could be an international one. Either way, the soundtrack of spring has changed, except for welcome cameos like today's. This saddens me, for not only are cuckoos extraordinary birds, they also add a unique atmosphere to wherever they call, just as church bells once echoed across the countryside and helped to define the land.

Here at The Patch, though, we are making gains as well as losses, and today's most exciting discovery unearths one of these. The usual singing Cetti's warbler was along The River next to The West Fields but then, at least 500 metres away, another one shouted. This doubles the number of singing males from one to two!

Yes, I know, this isn't on a par with finding a Dodo on your patch, or seeing a giant panda on your holiday, and perhaps the news underwhelms you and you'll think I'm a bit sad. But hey, you'll have your equivalent. Perhaps your treat is a new coffee shop opening on the street, or a new line of affordable and desirable clothes nearby, or you'll be stirred by a new song on the radio, or your heart leaps after a glance from an attractive stranger. But I heard a new Cetti's warbler today, and I'm as happy as Larry.

And besides, the Cetti's warbler has an intriguing status. This is still quite a rare bird in Britain, and before 1961 it had never been reliably recorded here at all. There were five records in England by 1970, so it was massively rare then, but the following year it began to breed, and since then it has become a regular British bird. It's still not that common, with about 700 singing males in Britain in an average year.

And not one, but TWO of them are here. Here's a toast to the annual census.

Monday 25 May 2009

There cannot ever have been a gentler invasion of Britain than this. For a few weeks our country was overwhelmed with nothing more than gossamer-soft wings, flapped by a butterfly with the soothing name of painted lady. It caused no alarms, and most of the public missed it, but it was arguably the wildlife event of the year.

I was already aware of the painted lady invasion by the time I witnessed it at The Patch, so to some extent its impact was blunted once I got here. I had spent a few days on the Dorset coast with the express purpose of showing people wildlife, including butterflies, so it would have been more than a little careless to miss seeing large, pale butterflies pass by at the rate of one every minute. That, of course, is the danger of leaving your patch vacant, even for the shortest time.

Today, though, almost three days after it began, this astonishing butterfly movement was obviously still in full swing, buoyed by the continuing southerly winds. Within a few moments of arriving at the edge of The Lake, I saw the first one go by. Thirty seconds later another made its way over the sun-glinting water, and many others followed in quick succession. A painted lady is a good sight at any time at The Patch, since there are only a handful of records each year. Thus, the most fleeting of visits would have confirmed that something special – indeed, extraordinary – was under way.

What does a butterfly invasion actually look like? It isn't quite what you might expect. I would have originally envisaged a dense mass of butterflies moving over the countryside like a cloud, rolling serenely along, the insects fluttering serendipitously in dense clusters over fields full of blooms. Witnessing such an invasion would have been like being caught in a warm snowfall of colourful, living flakes, partly settled and partly wafted by the breeze in no particular direction. In fact, it was nothing like that at all. The painted ladies weren't in a cloud, they were travelling along almost in single file, so that they made little impact on the landscape and it would have been easy to miss the scale of what was happening. Watching them was more like sitting beside the carriageway of a motorway at a quiet time, watching traffic hurtle by, each vehicle appearing in the distance as the previous one passed.

The only way one could actually appreciate the scale of what was happening was by counting. After five minutes I had seen seven painted ladies – hardly the stuff of a David Attenborough extravaganza – and after ten minutes I had fifteen. The rate actually slowed after that, and I managed seventeen in a quarter of an hour. However, if you were to extrapolate this, that would be sixty-eight an hour, and if they had carried on only for six hours, that would still be 408 in a day. The movement lasted for at least three days, which meant that a very conservative estimate of a thousand painted ladies passed over my one square kilometre Patch in May 2009. Incidentally, the papers reported that at least 10 million made landfall in Britain during the month.

What distinguished these painted ladies in the flesh was that they were going somewhere in a hurry. Of all the many that I saw, only a handful actually stopped to flutter distractedly at a flower-head for more than a moment. The rest powered by at head height, fluttering with confident, deep wing-beats – yet their occasional lurches to one side or another betrayed them as slightly out of control, as if their engines were revving just a little too much for comfort. It was easy to imagine that, somewhere to the north, there was a giant magnet pulling the painted lady population in that direction. Whatever was attracting them it was a powerful lure, irresistible even, and there must have been millions of individual butterflies in its thrall.

But what was luring them north? Nothing more, it seems, than destiny: the urge to colonize new places. The reason for the exceptional invasion was twofold: first, heavy early spring rains in North Africa had encouraged a spurt of growth in their favourite food plants, allowing the adults there to lay eggs in extraordinarily high numbers. Then, second, the hordes moved north because they are always compelled to do so each year as they expand their summer empire. With much higher numbers taking part than usual, more survived to reach as far as Britain.

As I mused on the extraordinary nature of the painted lady phenomenon, an individual actually paused a moment and landed at a nearby service station, a thistle. It just fluttered in and unhesitatingly began to drink, supping on several blooms in turn. It didn't look tired, just determined, and there was not a single blemish on its wings; it was no less marvellous a migrant than many of the birds that had been passing through The Patch in the previous few weeks. If the scientists tell it right, this very individual had probably begun its own journey in the Atlas Mountains of North Africa, and as it surged north at its peak it could have travelled 150 kilometres each day. With its bright combination of orange, black and white on the upper side of the wings, and an underside of dots, shading, lines and circles that would do justice to a mysterious treasure map, it looked every inch the exotic African insect.

Of the 10 million individuals that sped past the coasts of Britain, not one would have survived more than a few weeks. Travelling urges spent, each would have mated and the females would have found a thistle at the appointed time and laid their eggs. A month on, with a production schedule of almost unseemly haste rushing them through the larval and pupal stage, a new generation would then emerge to fill British fields again later in the summer, although few came to The Patch. Yet amazingly, come the autumn, only a tiny minority would fly back south, and an even tinier, recently discovered minority might overwinter. The rest would lay eggs, almost certainly doomed to perish during a British winter unsuited to these fair-weather visitors. With the onset of colder temperatures, the invasion would have fizzled out virtually to nothing. And only the memories of those who witnessed it would remain.

JUNE

Saturday 6 June 2009

If you are a keen watcher of one single area, let me ask you a question: how well do you know your patch? Do you know it in all its moods, all through the year and at all times of day?

The question arises because, however many times you might have visited, however many birds or animals you might have seen there and however thoroughly you think you have covered all corners to death, there might be one aspect of a patch you have never truly experienced. Be honest now. Have you ever stalked your patch at night?

If you are only a birdwatcher, night coverage of somewhere probably hasn't got on your radar. You might expect to hear an owl if you go in the late evening, and tick it off a year list. At night you might think you could possibly pick up the far-off calls of waders, such as whimbrels or greenshanks, which pass over in the hours of darkness during spring or autumn. In the autumn you could hear redwings or fieldfares passing over. But if you do, you will have to be content with birding by ear, and hearing just the odd fragments of snatched contact calls. You aren't going to see much.

If your interests extend to other wildlife, the idea of taking night trips should be more of a draw. After all, most British mammals are nocturnal, so it should be easier to encounter them in the hours of darkness, even if it's only the odd rustle or silhouette. But I have a feeling that most patch-watchers are distinctly reticent about going out at night, especially on their own, even if they know in their minds that the place they watch is likely to be safe. We humans are pretty diurnal, and even though our ancestors were probably used to going out at night, they would have learnt always to be watchful and on their guard.

This evening I decided to take a dedicated night walk, just for the hell of it. I wanted to be totally immersed in a midsummer night, immersed in a way only darkness could offer. Having made a short walk at the end of January on the edge of The Patch, I wanted to see the evening in and have a much longer exposure to the unlit outside world. After all, in a given year, our countryside is in darkness for half the time. To go only during the day is to short-change oneself.

So I left the comfort of my car at 9 p.m. and marched down to The South Side. I wanted to watch the sun go down and give myself the chance to see some mammals in the dusk. I had no plans, just nocturnal serendipity.

If you ever went to The Patch blindfolded, you could follow the regression of daylight with your ears, at least in spring. Just as birds wake up at different times for the dawn chorus, so they stop singing in a definite order to wind down the evening chorus. Great tits, for example, fall silent at just about sunset (and the singing males go to roost separately from the females on the nest), and chaffinches quieten down at about the same time. Wrens and dunnocks follow shortly afterwards, giving usually just a few bedtime bursts, and before long the airwaves are left to the thrushes and chats. I listened as a blackbird warbled its lustrous phrases with a slightly uninterested air, perhaps going through the motions, until falling silent. That left only the robin, the poor man's nightingale, shrilly to be the last bird standing as the gloom turned into genuine night.

While the small insectivorous birds settle down, so the small insectivorous mammals come out to play. Before the robin had finished, several bats ventured out and jinked over the path through Emily's Wood. Of course, in reality these insect hunters come out and replace the birdsong with their own racket; the only difference is that we cannot hear them. They are shouting out ultrasonic bursts that would sometimes have enough energy to burst our eardrums if we could detect them, but bats can make a place seem creepy, simply because of their apparent silence. I wonder how many people would find bats frightening if they could actually hear them?

On this evening I could hear the night-time racket, because I had brought a bat detector along. These are splendid bits of equipment, small hand-held gizmos which detect the echolocation signals of bats and 'translate' them in real time into equivalent, but audible frequencies. One of the enjoyable parts of bat detection is that the bats themselves don't generally talk in understandable phrases or sentences, but instead shoot out pulses of intense sounds, many of which sound like long, drawn-out farts (which quite naturally appeals to the child in us all). They can be hilarious, and they help us to realize just how much noise is made in the countryside during the night – it isn't quiet and peaceful at all. It's not just the bats, either; crickets and grasshoppers also make ultrasonic sounds which we completely miss with our own, limited ears. It makes one realize just how insensitive we humans are to what goes on around us.

There were at least three species of bats around. The ones that I could see in the gloaming were common pipistrelle bats, which are the most abundant species of bat in Britain. These mini mammals are voracious predators, and have been known to eat a thousand midges a night in just a few bouts of foraging, all of them caught using echolocation. Echolocation is one of nature's great marvels. The bats shoot out pulses of sounds with their mouths, and understand their world by means of the sound waves that reflect back to their ears (they aren't blind, but pipistrelles have very small eyes and probably don't use them much). This means that, in the dark, they are essentially gathering all their special awareness by hearing – and not direct hearing, either, but reflected sound signals. Scientists have shown that, while the echolocation is excellent for perceiving distance, it shouldn't in theory provide good detail about direction, so how on earth the bats manage to fly around so fast, and with such facility, is a complete mystery. They don't just appreciate their three-dimensional world, but actually manage to catch moving objects, too, which is simply astounding. They can appreciate the shape of flowers and leaves, and who knows what else?

Bats are mammals, but it is sobering to contemplate how utterly different from us they really are. They come out at night, they fly for a living, they hang upside down to rest, they perceive things with sounds we cannot hear. Yet as far as the natural world as a whole is concerned, we and they are quite closely related!

The other two species of bats around were the soprano pipistrelle and the noctule. This last is Britain's largest bat, and it was easy to make out with the naked eye as it flew over Samuel's Wood, flying with much slower wing-beats and more purposefully than its much smaller relative. Its early appearance in the evening, combined with its high flight, makes this species the sort of animal that even a birdwatcher can identify. This bat prefers bigger insect prey than paltry midges – indeed, there is a related species, the greater noctule, found in Europe, that actually plucks migrating birds out of the night sky.

As for the soprano pipistrelle, this animal is distinguished from the common pipistrelle by such minute details of lifestyle and behaviour that for hundreds of years nobody had any idea that there were two numerous species of pipistrelle in Britain. However, since the 1980s it has been shown that the soprano species calls differently; the strongest signal is at 55 kilohertz, as opposed to 45 kilohertz (although you might notice the dry humour in calling it 'soprano'). It might not seem much, but when you are a bat using echolocation, the frequency must be a major difference, affecting your whole life, and the language barrier would isolate the two types. It was also shown that the '45' and '55' pipistrelles use different colonies, have different genetics, slightly different muzzles and different fur and skin colours. The two are known as 'cryptic' species, whose distinctions defy our human perceptions of how creatures are different from one another.

There is one other distinction between the two cryptic species that is also worth a mention: the two species' penises are of different colours. It so happens that male members are big among bat enthusiasts (those members of the bats, I mean; can't speak for the humans), and they could almost be described as a hot topic. Put two bat specialists in a room, for example, and I absolutely guarantee that, assuming they talk shop, the word 'penis' will crop up within five minutes. Apart from segregating pips (as they are called), penises are also essential for distinguishing between the very similar Brandt's and whiskered bats, but I also wonder sometimes, in our cultural world where discussion of intimate matters of a physical nature is so controlled, or even suppressed, whether the liberal and unselfconscious declaration of the word 'penis' doesn't just make everybody feel better sometimes. We unfortunate birders don't have any such luxury, since apart from ostriches and ducks and a few other groups, birds don't have a penis at all, but merely a cloaca. It is an amusing thought as to how the bats might view this. Could birders and bat enthusiasts

be cryptic humans, whose distinctions defy the bats' perceptions of how creatures are different from one another?

It wasn't long before the silhouettes of bats were no longer
visible in the night sky, and darkness blotted out the familiarity of
The Patch. They say that, when a human being is exposed to the
dark for about half an hour, the eyes adjust and perform a lot
better than might be expected. No doubt it's true, but it still felt
very stygian and alien to me. I could manage the paths all right,
but the woods were so gloomy that they didn't look friendly at all,
and it wasn't too long until the experience became uncomfort-
able. My imagination took hold and I found myself fighting to
feel normal. Being alone in the dark, and at least a fifteen-minute
walk from the car, was turning out to be a potent experience.

You might think that hearing a rustling noise on the edge of
Samuel's Wood would have made matters worse, but in fact it
was oddly reassuring. I could tell that it wasn't a human being
(by far the least pleasant animal to meet in a dark place) because
it was coming from the ground. The animal was foraging just
out of sight, but from its slow pace but relatively substantial
disturbance I could tell that it was a badger. It was also close to
a known sett in Samuel's Wood. By sitting down I very much
hoped that I could get a glimpse of this magical carnivore,
having never seen one at The Patch before, but despite the
close encounter lasting several minutes the animal was clearly a
little wary, and not about to show itself.

Before the badger had slunk away back into the depths of the
wood, a shrill sound drifted gently over from the centre of The
Quarry. It was only a suggestion on the breeze at first, but soon
got louder and more obvious; then, just as quickly, it faded
away again. It was a succession of fast, high-pitched notes interspersed with slower, more insistent 'kree-a' ones: a classic song
flight from a little ringed plover. Of course, if you've read this
far you know that this species is The Patch's most unusual
breeding bird. On this June night, an individual clearly felt safe
enough to perform its circling song-flight. Quite a few waders

and other waterbirds make noisy flight displays at night in the comfort of predator-free darkness. Even a coot, the quintessence of an aerodynamically awkward bird that barely lifts itself off the water surface, will on occasion rise into the air and make an out-of-character trumpeting circuit, if the fancy takes it. It seems as though, for some birds, the low light intensity unleashes their inner self, and they are at last free to be demonstrative and noisy, like skinny-dipping human executives.

As if to prove the point, the little ringed plover was soon joined in its nocturne by another wader, a lapwing, one of a pair that was also holding territory on The Quarry and was probably incubating a clutch of eggs. If you've never heard a lapwing, the sound is a shrill whooping and whining, and it has the unmistakable whiff of unrestrained, quite inebriated joy and celebration. Just listening to a lapwing is captivating enough, but to listen to its duet with a little ringed plover on a starry June night on an unheralded piece of southern England, is a truly intoxicating experience.

The wader knees-up kept going into the night, long after I had got back to the car and driven home with an uplifted heart.

Wednesday 17 June 2009

I didn't expect to hear a cuckoo on The Patch on a warm mid-June afternoon. But having dismissed the possibility on first hearing, there was no doubt about the second bout of those unmistakable calls. It definitely wasn't somebody playing a joke, or at least, not unless they were perched up in the crown of a tree in Samuel's Wood. No, it was a real cuckoo, in the height of the breeding season.

Perhaps this is a sign that, for once, cuckoos have lingered on The Patch this year. After all, mid-June is the time when, suitably settled, they are said to change their tune (this, however, is nonsense, because they frequently sing variants on the 'cuckoo' theme right from the start of the singing season). For almost any other bird, hearing a song would be a virtually cast-iron breeding record. However, for this remarkable parasite, nothing is ever simple. Males, which are the ones that make the song, don't actually hold a defended territory, so there is nothing to rule out this bird being simply a passer-by trying its luck. But then, on the other hand, the females, which actually do hold territories, can be extremely unobtrusive, so without seeing a female actually present, or coming across a juvenile being fed by its hosts, one cannot be sure.

Cuckoos have good reasons to be unobtrusive. Not only do they need to be very sneaky when approaching a nest in which to lay their eggs, but they also need to keep a low profile throughout their stay in the breeding season. Small birds almost invariably mob cuckoos when they find them, some-times actually attacking, so the cuckoo needs to live its life permanently undercover.

For many birds on The Patch, the sound of a cuckoo might bring a chill, but this is no longer a significant threat, for the eggs of their first brood have already hatched. This has clearly been a good year for the local pied wagtails, which are occa-sional cuckoo hosts, because youngsters of this species are everywhere. And around the shores of The Lake, they are feeding on an effective insect bonanza. The hot weather has meant that the countryside is boiling over with invertebrate productivity, and I see no fewer than eleven pied wagtail juve-niles in one spot tucking into an unusual delicacy: common blue damselflies. So many of these powder-blue insects, with their feeble fairy-like flight and stick-like bodies, have hatched from the waterside vegetation that the pied wagtails, normally so busy and fidgety when feeding, are simply standing still and waiting for the insects to float towards them. One bird takes five damselflies in as many minutes, each one a large meal for such a small bird. Goodness, these wagtails are so preoccupied that they have actually forgotten to wag their tails.

The insect bloom is obvious on the farmland to the west of The Shire Field, where a large flock of rooks has gathered to forage the afternoon away. It has clearly been a decent breeding season for the colony that lives less than a couple of kilometres to the north of The Patch; compare today's count of 224 birds with the pre-breeding sixty-five that I counted back in January. Judging by previous counts there are eighty or so rooks in the breeding colony, forty pairs, so the figures suggest that each pair has raised an average of 3.6 young, which would be extremely impressive – in fact, pretty much capacity. So perhaps there are some visitors from another colony here.

Whatever their provenance, the rooks are feasting well. Everywhere I look, there is a bird digging up a meal from the grass-covered soil, and equally everywhere I look there is a youngster begging from an adult, flapping its wings in baby fashion and opening its beak, gaping in anticipation. In fact the youngsters are very well grown and almost identical to their parents, distinguishable only by the fact that their bills and face are not yet dirty-white; they look a bit old still to be begging for food, so are probably just being lazy. The scene has the appearance of a very large picnic, so gentle and busy does it look – a picnic for parents and children where polite conversation is interspersed with practised attention for needy progeny. And it is equally noisy; the begging youngsters making somewhat wheezy efforts at a caw, the adults almost purring. As the birds feed they are shambling across the field with their slightly rolling gait, which always denies rooks the sinister appearance of crows, which run or walk menacingly. And of course, since carrion crows nest singly, they are never seen in large, benign family gatherings like this.

The humming productivity of the rook nursery is the result of months of hard effort in difficult conditions. This colony has come a long way from the chilly days of January, when the pairs first began to refurbish their nests in preparation for breeding. The females will have laid eggs as early as March, before the leaves were on the trees, and when the treetops must have been very exposed. The incubation, which usually lasts about sixteen days, will also have been work for a hardy species. But the rook begins its breeding season unusually early for a good reason – the young subsist on worms and other soft-bodied invertebrates. These animals are a good deal easier to dig out during the spring, when the weather is wet and the soil moist – any later and the earth will dry out and drive worms deeper into the ground. Thus the rooks time their breeding to coincide with convenient feeding conditions. Incidentally, breeding early in the season also compels them to court and pair up at an unusual time – they do it in October and November.

Another early breeder whose young have spilled out of the nest is the grey heron, and today there are seven individuals around The Quarry, the highest number of the year. Not surprisingly, most of them are juveniles, recognizable by lacking the adults' neat black plume-stripe that begins behind the eye and drapes down from the neck; instead the crown is dull grey, making them look as though they are wearing a cap. Juvenile herons have the same capacity as the adults to stand hunched next to the water, neck sunk into shoulders, and to look irredeemably fed up, as if they have just turned up at a fish and chip shop and found it closed. I don't suppose they really are grumpy, but they don't provide the best advertisement for heron-hood. Nobody is quite sure why herons nest so early in the year – they can lay eggs in February – but it might be for similar reasons to the rook. When the young are in the nest, it is probably easier for the adults to catch the fish and frogs that they need before the vegetation has grown too lush and tall, offering their prey extra concealment. Another possibility, which could just be a by-product of the first reason, is that an early season allows these youngsters plenty of time to learn to catch prey before it becomes a more difficult prospect in the winter months. If your patch includes a wetland you will probably be aware of L-plated juvenile herons and the sheer incompetence that they often display. I have seen them falling into the water when trying to snatch a fish, and have equally seen them trying to hunt from ridiculous positions, such as from a raft over deep water, from which they couldn't reach a fish if they had a neck like a flamingo. The adults don't spend any time teaching their progeny and, quite frankly, it's a wonder that any of them survive at all.

Mind you, if these youngsters were sensible they could always catch a few passing insects. Today has seen something of a bloom of dragonflies: not just the common blue damselflies upon which the pied wagtails were feasting, but azure damselflies and banded demoiselles are everywhere, too. It's a good afternoon for a trip down to the sluggish River, where the June vegetation is running riot, plants of all kinds competing for space, like those crowds of people you see fringing the route of a marathon. There are pompously tall yellow irises, crowded reeds, foam-topped meadowsweet, nettles, all kinds of grasses, bulrushes and some cow-parsley lookalikes called water-drop-worts, while the edge of The River is clogged with water-lilies, pondweed and duckweed. The diversity is doubtless trumped by any tropical forest, but this corner of high summer England takes some beating for sheer luxuriance.

A couple of interesting damselflies and dragonflies can be sought out next to The River, especially on fine days like this. One of them is the white-legged damselfly, the sort of insect that you definitely wouldn't hire as a bouncer; it is the defini-tion of frail and fragile, or simply weedy if you prefer. These insects are almost like flying gossamer threads in the way that they seem to float in the breeze, and although technically powder blue they look whiter in colour than most damselflies, too, with one (male) or two (female) black lines running down the abdomen. These porcelain-like miniatures cannot cope with much more than a gentle breeze, and they usually swarm around ranks of chunky plant stems, such as nettle-beds. They perch with their wings held out at about forty-five degrees, in contrast to most damselflies, which at rest hold theirs over the back, and the males have eponymous white legs, which they dangle irresistibly when performing courtship flights over the females, which presumably get all hot and sticky when they see the performance. This species is confined to the warmer, southern parts of the British Isles, and even here it is highly localized, being found only in areas free of pollution. So their presence is a good measure of the quality of The River.

Our other unusual odonate is the scarce chaser, another species with a light blue body, at least in the male, as well as a very small black tip to the abdomen. It is one of the very few dragonflies or damselflies in which the female, with its orange body tipped by a black line than gets broader towards the tail, is actually more distinctive than the male. It's a dragonfly as opposed to a damselfly, being thick-bodied and holding its wings out from its body, rather than over its back, at rest, and is typically aggressive, the male spending much time defending a small clump of waterside from its male rivals. This species only occurs in a 'few river systems with lush floodplains' according to my dragonfly book, which means that The Patch, as far as this creature is concerned, is one of those special areas in Britain.

There are other dragonflies about, including black-tailed skimmers and emperor dragonflies, all shimmering wings and exotic names. These dragonflies, as opposed to damselflies, are the truly turbo-charged insects, fast-moving and fast-living, insects with superb eyesight and razor-sharp jaws, big killers and zealous lotharios. They have been heated by the sun into an obsessive afternoon of abundant food and ripe possibilities for sex, and they tear this way and that over the swaying reed tops and glinting waters, all abuzz.

Up above them – high above – fly two hobbies, circling ominously, riding the thermals. These predatory birds, which catch all their food in flight, specialize in dragonflies. They watch the frenzy and await their chance.

JULY

Tuesday 7 July 2009

It's shaping into a seriously wet summer. The sky's face is set in grey and the tears seem to be falling every day. It's even cold at times, with a stiff wind. Every visit to The Patch coincides with raindrops on The Lake and on The Quarry's pools, and usually a hastened exit.

Today is no different, and in addition to the driving rain, the swifts too are falling from the skies. Normally these birds feed higher up than their fellow aerial feeders – swallows at head height, sand martins at street-light height, house martins at rooftop height and, well above all of them, commanding the heavens, the swifts, the ones that can wheel at top speed in the fresh air, free from obstacles. But today they have been brought down, if not to earth, at least towards it. They are still flying with swooping confidence, but they have pitched down to just a metre or two above the ground or, more especially, skimming over the surface of The Lake, together with their aerial underlings. Taking a look at the lead-grey waves I can see that there are small bodies skimming from left to right, right to left, snatching the insects that are hatching directly from the water.

I have mentioned before about the swifts' need to concentrate their feeding near the water surface in bad weather. But
there is something unusual about today's 'fall' of swifts – the
sheer number of individuals involved. Swallows and both
martins breed at The Patch and the local birds are present in
small numbers. But there are hundreds of swifts here today,
perhaps three or four hundred, and I know of no breeding sites
nearby. I doubt whether there are three hundred breeding
swifts within a thirty-kilometre radius.

So their multitudes require explanation. It is an extraordinary
one, tied in closely with the weird biology of the common swift.
And on a rainy afternoon, it is worth dwelling on for a while.

Sometimes we birders forget that the swift is an extreme
specialist. It is a sensationally efficient flier, not requiring to
land at all for at least the first two years of life, from the time
that it first leaves the nest to the time that it claims a nest-site
of its own as an adult. But this expertise doesn't confer upon
the swift command of all kinds of niches plump with food;
instead it gives it access to a very particular foraging space and
food supply, the so-called 'aeroplankton'. This term refers to
the multitude of wind-borne insects and other invertebrates
that can be found drifting high above ground during the
summer; most are flying insects such as aphids and small moths,
but others, remarkably, are tiny spiders that ride on strands of
web like parachutes. These creatures are caught in the breeze
close to the ground and whisked up into the atmosphere,
programmed to land in some far-off spot where they can make
their home. It's their way of dispersal. The summer air could be
seen, therefore, as its usual mixture of nitrogen, oxygen and
water vapour, together with pollen, dust and a host of flying
creatures in suspension.

If the weather is warm and settled, swifts have no trouble
feeding. But when low pressure crosses the country, bringing
rain and wind, it has a profound effect on the swifts' food supply.

Even when the meteorological low is still 500 kilometres away, swifts already notice a drop in plankton density. When the low has arrived, they have trouble feeding, and must resort to visiting water-bodies. But when conditions are really dire, and it looks as though there will be no food around for a day or more, the swifts do something still more remarkable – they simply evacuate the area. When a big area of unsettled weather approaches, some swifts will actually fly around the low, taking a short-cut (usually to the south-west) to meet the better weather. A swift may travel as much as 1,000 kilometres, simply to ride the low like a boat can ride out a wave on the ocean.

The most astonishing aspect of these midsummer 'escape movements' is that, at least sometimes, breeding birds – parents – take part in them. Imagine that. One day a breeding swift is catching food for its youngster in an area of southern England; the next day that same parent has taken an away day in continental Europe, perhaps as far as Germany, leaving its youngster or youngsters behind. Not surprisingly, the swift chicks, adapted to an unreliable food supply, are resistant to starvation, and are able to lower their own metabolic rate to become torpid.

Who knows, therefore, where the swifts over The Lake today have come from? It could be from a completely different part of Britain, or even from the Continent. These birds are great travellers. The sky is big, and knows no borders.

Great Birding Days

Thursday 23 July 2010

On a spot where fifteen years ago one could stand on solid ground, in a field similar to all the others around here, and where twelve months ago there was an empty, gravel-bottomed shell dotted with small puddles cowering under the July heat, today there is a duck nursery, a burst of babyhood.

And it's not just the mallards, which always hid their nests in the unshaven tangles by the side of The River, nor even gadwalls, which used to unearth broods here from time to time in the past, incubated in some mysterious Atlantis-like breeding refuge that I never discovered, but tufted ducks. They have exploded here reproductively, and now the broods of chicks litter The New Lake like small floating bundles of ash debris. The dark brown ducklings, no more than a day or two out of the egg, bob around their mothers, inherently curious and willing to range, yet prone to sudden bursts of that classic duckling Keystone Cops panic when they go too far. I am astonished, upon counting them, that there are no fewer than nine families represented here. Some mothers have just one or two chicks, but two of them string eight along behind them, and altogether there are fifty-four recent additions to the tufted duck population.

This is extraordinary for a couple of reasons. First, tufted ducks have never bred here before. The species is quite a fussy one, with a need for just the right depth of water and just the right amount of safe waterside vegetation, and the most we see in summer is a small group of dozy non-breeders with nothing on their minds but a new set of feathers. An acceleration from nought to fifty-four in a season is pretty impressive. And second, the tufted duck is quite a scarce breeding bird in Britain as a whole. Most birdwatchers cannot realize this when they see the black-and-white business-suited males and chocolate-brown females covering lakes and ponds in winter profusion. But the British population, numbering up to 12,000 pairs, is much smaller than that of, say, the sparrowhawk, and vastly less than that of the puffin. It might be overdoing the statistics to call them rare, but they are special, and today they are adorning The Patch in resplendent bounteousness.

Their presence here is surprisingly descriptive of the state of The New Lake. You might not be able to judge a book by its cover, but you can read a water-body by the state of its covering of wildfowl. The presence of tufted ducks, for example, is a pretty reliable clue that a lake has substantial areas of water over two metres deep, and that it is not overly clogged with weeds and other vegetation. It will also tell you that there is plenty of productivity; sunlight is getting through to the bottom and a healthy flora and fauna are being supported. And third, the fish population, especially of the larger, grazing species, is under control. Tufted ducks don't cope as breeding birds with competition from big fish, because there simply isn't enough food to go round. On this New Lake the fish are coming in through pipes fed by a nearby river (not *The* River), and as they grow up they will probably render the habitat unsuitable for tufties.

Incidentally, in the winter the presence of certain other ducks is also indicative of The New Lake's ecology. On the simplest level, a good population of gadwalls, shovelers or pochards means that the water is fresh, rather than salty. And the more shovelers, the more you can be sure that some areas of the water are shallow, because these birds prefer to feed in water that is a metre deep or less. The presence of wigeons on a fresh-water lake usually means that there is somewhere to graze, usually on the sides where grass can grow. Wigeons are, when all is said and done, a little like flying sheep: they are specialist grazers, highly sociable and they don't like dogs. The latter's presence hereabouts must drive the wigeons mad.

Anyway, back to tufted ducks. The fifty-four young are a bit special, and my suspicion is that the species will never again successfully produce progeny in such numbers. Today, then, could be a moment in The Patch's history that proves to be unique. I'm very glad that I was here to witness it.

Tuesday 27 July 2010

You won't hear too many people in the street getting excited about it; indeed, you won't find all that many natural history enthusiasts getting excited about it either. But then, what do you expect from a population who watch *Coronation Street*? The months of June and July witness something genuinely exciting and eye-opening: the zenith of the moth season in Britain. While the world stays in and watches soap operas, there is treasure flying around out there to be admired by anyone who looks.

'The moth season?' you might ask, aghast. What is there to admire about moths? Moths are insects that eat clothes and flutter idiotically towards light bulbs, showing about as much control and spatial awareness as a Volvo driver. The way they flutter is disturbing, and when they stop fluttering they are brown and boring. What could possibly be interesting about moths?

Well, those same, boring moths – admittedly not at their best when flying around light bulbs – are, I can tell you, a sheer marvel. Large yellow underwings, for example, are known to be able to orientate themselves by means of the rotation of the stars. Moths can travel thousands of kilometres, across land and sea, using nothing more than their own onboard computer. Moths can hear the approach of their arch-predators, bats, and duck out of the way. They can smell pheromones across hundreds of metres and swarm to the signal of siren females. Not bad for a mere insect, eh? Moths are amazing, and mysterious, and pretty cool.

Whatever their behavioural attributes, however, this diary entry is not going to enthuse entomologically over anything other than the empirical diversity of moths. I admit I have been an evangelist for moth appreciation for many years, and I have found that nothing makes people sit up and listen more than the realization of the miracle of moth diversity that is found in their backyard. Let me give you some figures first: most gardens in Britain, at least away from the coldest, most windswept and more mountainous parts of the country, will play host to about two hundred species in the course of the year, and others will host many more. My own garden, not very far from The Patch, has just hoisted the 300-species marker – and that's only the larger species, the so-called 'macro-moths'. This, you will appreciate, is serious diversity.

Now, the truth is that most gardens will also host a similar number of species of flies, too, and probably more beetles, but there is a genuine reason why moths are a more exciting bio-diversity marvel than these other groups. To study beetles and flies you need a lot of persistence and a hand-lens to tell the difference between species, but the naked eye can distinguish moths with ease. Yes, many species are in shades of brown, but many others exhibit bright, even brilliant coloration, enough to rival butterflies (which are, incidentally, nothing more than day-flying moths). And, glory be, there are inexpensive books to help you work them all out. Moths are a blessing for all, waiting to be enjoyed.

Personally, while I have been running a non-lethal moth trap in the garden for a decade or so, I had never managed to do so in The Patch before. This was for the simple reason that moth traps require 240 volts to run them, and The Patch is not overrun with mains electricity. However, on this evening I brought along a secret weapon: a fellow enthusiast called Ray Cook, and his generator. On this warm July night we planned to run two traps into the early hours of the morning.

What was exciting about this – and often is when it comes to moths – is that we would be trapping in virgin territory. To our knowledge, nobody had ever run a moth trap in this area before, so everything we found would represent a discovery of sorts. Okay, it's not New Guinea or an Andean valley or some-thing, where one might catch something new to science. But it was still a case of pioneering in backyard Britain, mothing where no men had mothed before. And furthermore, with its wide variety of habitats – riverside, woodland, farmland, grass-land – I had already formed the impression that The Patch was Moth Heaven waiting to be discovered.

Thus, it was with genuine excitement that we made our way in cars past the hallowed gates that protect The Water Works and on towards The River on The South Side, our traps primed for glory. Solemnly, Ray carried the generator and placed it on the path between Emily's Wood and The Marsh. By running cables, Ray's trap was set up close to the riverside vegetation, while mine stood close to the edge of the wood, and in that way we had a chance of catching a real variety of species. Thus armed, we waited for the dusk to fade into darkness.

At this point I had better explain the workings of moth traps, because they are very different from the insect traps seen in bars and restaurants that make loud clicks as they electrocute their visitors. An entomological moth trap consists of a box made of light metal, or a plastic drum, which forms the bulk of the trap, upon which is placed a very bright mercury vapour bulb that attracts moths and other insects by dint of throwing out strong ultraviolet and also visible light. The moths are attracted and disoriented by the beam, as is their wont, and tend to fly in circles or semicircles towards the bulb, whereupon they stumble through a narrow opening in the top of the trap below the bulb and find themselves inside the drum or box. All moth people fill the bowels of the trap with open egg-boxes, which simulate the feel of bark or other rough plant surfaces, and provide a place for the captured insects to rest. The moths then calm down and can be examined. In practice, enthusiasts usually place a white sheet below a working trap, where many moths tumble prior to entering the trap itself. It is often easy to identify a species here before it enters the trap and, if it needs careful examination by daylight to confirm the record, it can be boxed and kept until release the next day.

You might be surprised to learn that moths, despite the heightened number of species, require just as much patience to enjoy as birds do. Ray and I stood for quite a long time before we registered very much fluttering around the traps. Instead we watched the last of the light-dance reflect off the surface of The

River, which eventually faded into a turgid, inky black. A light cloud of mist rose gently over the fields on the opposite side of The River, and the trees in Emily's Wood turned from tired green to dark shapes looming over the path. I could claim to you that we breathed in the glorious scents of night-time July – fresh grass and the like – but in truth if we had done that we would have choked on a mass of black caddis flies. These moth-like insects were everywhere, swarming in clouds around the traps, so that a gnarled veteran like Ray, whose moth career spans fifty years and has coped with catching insects in mountains, bogs and deep forests, could barely manage to get within two metres of the lights. For the uninitiated, caddis flies are insects with four wings that are hairy rather than scaled, they hold the wings in a tent-like posture over their body, they lack a proboscis, and – I can tell you – they taste a little bit like Ryvita. Before long there were probably a thousand around each trap.

Eventually the moths did come, just about managing to make their way through the vast swarms of caddis flies, no doubt bumping and weaving and having to say 'excuse me' every few seconds. The first arrival was a dingy footman, not quite starting the proceedings off with a charismatic bang. It's a dull grey moth, a sort of common gull to a birder, appreciated only by a true enthusiast; the most exciting thing about a dingy footman is that its larvae eat lichens: hot stuff, eh? It was followed by a character with an intriguing name and an even more intriguing lifestyle – the ghost moth. This species gets its name from the male's habit of seemingly floating above the grass, swaying gently from side to side (not sure that ghosts actually do this, but never mind). The males gather together in groups of up to about fifty to attract the females, a bit like a strip troupe, and each of them does this swaying hover and also releases a scent at the same time. And then, just like in the ads, the scent proves irresistible to the females and they come flying in. Not standing on ceremony – the females sometimes just barge the males and both fall into the grass, where the inevitable takes place. This steamy episode is the zenith of the moths' life: since neither sex has a proboscis, they don't even feed in the adult stage. Sex is everything. It could be said, therefore, that being plunged into a light trap or swept into a butterfly net was probably not what our ghost moths had in mind for the evening.

After a few minutes a special visitor came into the trap, a ruby tiger. You will guess that this species is deep red, and so it is; it's the sort of moth that naturalists hope will be attracted in at a public moth-trapping event so that the uninitiated can admire its colours (it's hard to get visitors excited by a moth called a lead-coloured drab, for example). However, even allowing for its impressive coloration, which means that it rivals many a butterfly for good looks, the ruby tiger is a moth megastar for a quite different reason. This backyard moth has an astonishing survival technique – it can 'tell' a potentially predatory bat to leave it alone, because it is distasteful. This little insect, which genuinely does taste unpleasant, actually makes bursts of clicks within the bat's ultrasonic range, a message that the bat can hear and understand. So when a bat is approaching a ruby tiger, it knows to avoid it. And because the ruby tiger is a widespread and common moth, you can bet that this incredible invertebrate–mammal exchange takes place within the airspace of many a suburban garden, even yours.

Soon The Patch outside fell into darkness, and our trap bulbs made a psychedelic bubble of extreme brightness that began to attract a higher number and variety of moth species. As each one came in, Ray and I would take a look and agree on the species, speaking out a succession of evocative names, as if we were reading from one of the more way-out fashion catalogues. One of the corollary delights of taking an interest in moths is learning those names, many of them conferred upon their subjects by groups of inebriated Victorian men of letters and the cloth. Some are long and unwieldy: within minutes we were visited by a lesser broad-bordered yellow underwing and a dark-barred twin-spot carpet; others poetic, such as heart and dart and the dog's tooth, both named for the patterns on their forewings. Some moth names are plain ridiculous; one of the common species that turned up tonight goes by the name of the uncertain. It very closely resembles several other species, and so the enthusiast is forever not sure which one it is, thus the tease of the name. Somebody, it is clear, had a great deal of fun with these names. Anybody fancy a night of whisky and naming a few thousand beetles?

Not every night is a good moth night – and there are plenty of variables, including temperature, the amount of moonlight and the heaviness of the atmosphere, that affect the number of moths that fly – and the truth is that the first couple of hours were a little bit slow. We ate caddis flies to pass the time, and recalled past memories of great moths, until, just after midnight, the insects at last began to reward us for our efforts. That's not because we suddenly ran into a parade of colourful and unusually marked moths; as regular entomologists that happens all the time. No, instead we began to catch some rarer and habitat-specific species, the sort to make specialists purr, even if their charms might be lost on the casual passer-by. Thus, for example, we caught a double kidney. Despite sounding like a very unfortunate condition, this is a pretty scarce moth with – well I never – two pale kidney marks on each grey-brown forewing. It is attached to marshy places, with the larvae feeding on sallows and black poplar. We also caught several of a species called the crescent, a brick-coloured moth with a strange white mark on each wing that looks like the lobes of an ear. And then there were the wainscots, the quintessential moths of reed-beds and wet areas, whose larvae feed on marshy plants and provide food for such choice birds as reed warblers and bearded tits. The brown-veined wainscot caterpillar feeds on the leaves of the common reed and the bulrush wainscot larvae nosh on the leaves and stems of – guess what? With the crescent taking the leaves of yellow iris, and other species of marshy moths feeding on different species of wet-loving plant, the sheer joy of biodiversity and the intricate subtlety of how it all weaves together just makes one want to jump up and down in ecstasy.

And this is not all, for the moths also have a life to live during the daytime. Not only do they have different coloured and shaped caterpillars which live on different sorts of leaves, and not only do they have different lifestyles and flight periods and different times in the night when they usually fly, and not only do they have different places to feed and different migratory patterns, which is amazing enough – they also have different hiding places during the day. And this feature helps to explain why, albeit sometimes subtly, they all have different patterns on the wings. Some choose to hide in grass, others in leaf-litter, others on the bark of trees. One of the moths that Ray and I caught, the lime-speck pug, looks exactly like a small lump of bird excreta – and no predator is going to be attracted to that. Most, though, simply go for concealment, being clad in an endless variety of different patterns for different parts of the vegetation.

Thus, one of the miracles of moth diversity is that the patterns of these nocturnal creatures' wings are actually designed for daytime viewing – or not viewing. Incredible.

And the next time you dismiss a moth for just being brown, remember that fact.

AUGUST

Monday 10 August 2009

It's August and the relative birding doldrums of midsummer have given way to salivation at the prospect of good times ahead. The birds have largely finished breeding and all over the country, every birdwatcher everywhere has started to notice the shifting of parameters. The birds aren't on their territories any more, which means that everything is moving about. And that means that pretty much anything can turn up anywhere. It will be like that from now until at least the middle of November, a thought that makes me almost giddy with delight. Thank the Good Lord for the autumn migration, the natural, unpredictable postal service that brings a fresh delivery of birds almost every day.

I go out today with a hat-trick in mind, three delightful birds that I haven't yet seen at The Patch this year but all of which are typical August migrants. Most migrants have peak times for their appearance, and mark the passage of the season; for example, willow warblers dominate from mid-August to mid-September, but after this they decline in number and are overtaken by their close relatives, chiffchaffs. It happens that the next two or three weeks will be hot for garden warblers and pied flycatchers, and although the redstart peaks a little later, there is no reason not to look for this species now.

These three species cannot be guaranteed on The Patch. None of them have the right habitat to breed here, and for some reason that I have never been able to fathom, they don't make frequent touch-downs even in The Patch's woods, hedgerows and thickets. Indeed, it is a source of minor irritation that, so far, I have never seen a pied flycatcher at The Patch at all. Actually, for irritation read embarrassment and frustration. Just about every patch-birder in the whole country has seen at least one pied flycatcher on their site; read the blogs and reports, and the August bushes of Britain are alive with these blue-tit-sized, white-fronted and dark-brown-backed birds, with their wide white wing-bars. They are quite common and they migrate on what is called a broad front, meaning that, rather than following a particular path during their migration, they simply set off and follow a heading – south, or south-west, for example. There is therefore no reason at all why pied flycatchers shouldn't pass by every year. And just to compound the puzzle, at the edge of my garden, not far north of The Patch, I have a little birch and willow copse that currently hosts three.

Today, then, has got to be the day. The migrants are around, the weather is fine; all I have to do is turn up. There will be orange tails flicking, there will be small brown and white mites sallying, and there will be brown, featureless warblers gobbling the first of the elderberries. Redstart, pied flycatcher and garden warbler, here I come.

You know what's coming, don't you? Of course I flog The Patch for several hours, getting hot, bothered and more and more frustrated. Emily's Wood is the quintessential flycatcher stopover – nothing; The Thicket has had redstarts in the past several times – nothing; the newly grown bushes around The Lake are a perfect garden warbler restaurant – nothing. My log for hours of birding reads: one common whitethroat, one willow warbler heard calling, one chiffchaff. The trip is a complete let down. The strong optimism that I had at the start is initially diluted, then strained away and then burned up by the bird-less landscape, leaving a waste of despair. There isn't a flicker of life. The truth is that, when a patch is bad, it is really bad. And when, like mine, it is an inland site, a trip of this sort is purgatory.

Why do days like this happen? There has to be a biological reason and, of course, the simple one is that the birds have not found it expedient to make a stop at The Patch. This could be either because they are not moving or, more likely, because they *are* migrating but the clear skies have allowed them to clear out.

On inland sites it can be extraordinarily difficult to read the weather. On some patch-watchers' blogs you read things like: 'The wind shifted to the south-west and, as expected, 28 Manx shearwaters flew past the Head'. But on my (inland) Patch of unheralded habitat, without any major topographical feature, such as a coastline or high ground, it becomes much more difficult to read the charts and predict what might be around. Even after eight years of watching, all I know for certain is that poorer weather, such as rain or winds, is likely to move birds and make things happen.

In the early days of the great migration lift-off, however, I still can't predict what will happen – except that there will be plenty of blank and frustrating days like this.

Tuesday 11 August 2009

I needed to get out today to check that there is some life in The Patch. As it turned out, there was a lot more life than yesterday, a fact that confirms the perversity of wildlife-watching: same place, same weather, same observer, different outcome. I lucked into a large flock of birds alongside the edge of Samuel's Wood, all of them feeding actively in the oaks, beeches and alders. It was good to see leaves that were dripping with birds instead of this year's constant raindrops.

There weren't any headline names; just lots of everything. And the flock was satisfyingly symptomatic of the passage of the year. Each of the several species involved – long-tailed, blue and great tits, treecreepers, willow warblers and chiffchaffs – had a story to tell, just by being part of the group. I will explain.

Let's take the blue tits and great tits first. In the flock there were about twenty-five of each species present, and every individual bore the yellow-stained cheeks of youth (adults of both species have white cheeks). That meant that, unless The Patch's pairs (about four of each) had been producing pretty much to capacity, which is very unlikely in a wet, miserable summer, most of these birds would not have been products of the immediate area, but visitors from outside. They were youthful interlopers, but from where?

What happens when young birds leave the nest is that, after a short period of aftercare from their parents (usually just a few days in the case of tits), they are effectively booted out. It is necessary for them to leave home, if you will, because staying around could potentially cramp the parents' style, overburden the area and, in the very worst cases, lead to inbreeding in future seasons. So the youngsters begin to wander; they leave the near vicinity of the parents' wood and might travel, for example, merely a kilometre or two, sometimes more. Broods also split up. Once they have some flight time behind them, they will suss out their new surroundings for a potential territory next year, and they will learn the ropes of being whatever species they are. Interestingly, part of the latter process involves joining what is effectively an adolescent flock (which is what I was watching today on The Patch). These flocks move about a neighbourhood, sticking together so that plenty of eyes are open for spotting predators, while each hones its particular foraging techniques, both individual and species-specific. Individuals are known to watch and observe other members of the flock, picking up tips about effective foraging, building up a portfolio of niche-hunting experience. So today, for example, I could see all of the young blue tits feeding in the upper canopy of the oaks, often right on the end of branches, while many of the young great tits were foraging on the tree-trunks, and some descended to the ground.

These adolescent flocks are very much a feature of late summer. At night every individual blue or great tit roosts alone, but in the morning it listens to the calls of peers and joins the flock for most of the day. Later on, in September, both young-sters and adults, all unrelated, will form similar roaming flocks of flexible membership, and they will persist for much of the coming winter.

The situation with long-tailed tits is quite different. In today's flock most of the birds present are clearly juveniles – each looking as though it has dipped its head in chocolate – but there are adults present, too (a white face with a broad dark line over the eye). In this species the youngsters are not booted out of the territory, but actually remain by their parents' side right into the autumn. Indeed, the young males stay in the family territory until next spring, while juvenile females are exchanged with unrelated units in the course of the winter. The difference is explained by the roosting behaviour of long-tailed tits. These small-bodied birds huddle together to roost, and so the family unit is a less stressful quorum to huddle in than would be a gathering of unrelated birds.

The origin of the single treecreeper in the flock is less easy to ascertain. Adult treecreepers, unlike blue or great tits, tend to remain on their territory all year round, so the individual may well have been one of the two pairs that breed on The Patch. Equally, juvenile treecreepers wander in the same way as young blue and great tits, so the bird might equally have been from outside.

Finally, the ten or so willow warblers and chiffchaffs that were sharing the treetops with the tits have, I am sure, a quite different origin. There are a couple of pairs of chiffchaffs on The Patch, but no breeding willow warblers, so these individuals are likely to be from much further away. People often don't realize that a lot of British birds begin their southward migration much earlier than expected, some of them even before July is over. So the willow warblers could be from northern England, or even Scotland. Theirs is a leisurely journey maintained by short steps; and one of those steps has brought them here, on nothing more than a temporary stopover.

Whatever their origin though, and whatever their future, be it a trip to tropical Africa or a flight of just a kilometre to a new territory, all these birds are united here in a cohesive flock for a day. They share the same branches, darting from one to the next, gleaning insects from July's hardening leaves, watching out for communal danger. For today their interests and fears are shared; tomorrow it will be a different story.

Tuesday 18 August 2009

It isn't possible to walk around The Lake at present without noticing the goldfinches. They are everywhere, and it seems as though I cannot walk more than a few metres without disturbing small parties of them from in front of me, as if they were colourful locusts in plague proportions. The majority of them are exploiting a large patch of common knapweed by the northern end of The Lake, where there is a wide verge between the water and the hedgerow that marks the edge of The Lane. The knapweed is at its peak, each stiff-stemmed plant crowned with a Bart Simpson haircut of alarming purple, below which a hard head of bracts provides great feeding for birds with a taste for seeds and a lot of dexterity. The plants provide a rich purple stain, making a sharp contrast to the tired green of the bushes behind.

Today there are no fewer than eighty goldfinches in this

corner. They are all clinging on to the knapweed heads with their strong feet, but not having an easy time – clearly the harvesting of the seeds is far from straightforward. Every now and again the goldfinches have to flutter to keep their balance, revealing their brilliant yellow wing-bars, and when several are doing this at once it is a feast of colour to the eye. The bracts of the knapweed protect the seeds well, but goldfinches are superbly adapted to meet the task of excising them. Not only do the birds have athletic balance, they also have very narrow bills that are easy to insert between the tightly packed bracts. Another neat adaptation is the goldfinch's jaw muscles. They have the strength to shut the bill and crack open the kernel of the seed inside the palate, but in addition these little seed-eaters also have unusually strong muscles to open the bill. This means that they can insert their bill into the overlapping scales and, by the act of opening it, can wrench the bracts apart, releasing the seed, which is then scooped up by the tongue.

The goldfinches might be working hard, but they cannot, it seems, stop themselves twittering; it's as if, in the boredom of their foraging, they need the equivalent of listening to a chirpy radio broadcast. The sound is a silvery, sweet-voiced medley of mellifluous and harsh notes, based on a motif sounding like 'tickle-it' and when several birds are singing at once the chorus brings to mind the trickling of a mountain stream.

Or maybe I'm being fanciful. But that's the thing about goldfinches. They are the Christmas decorations among birds, the glitz and shimmer. Yet they don't look tacky, either; they are almost invariably well turned out. They could almost be called the perfect bird – common, tame, colourful and easy on the ear. They refute the (albeit absurd) notion that British birds are generally colourless compared to tropical birds (do you know how many brown species there are in the Tropics?), and they delight both hard-core birdwatchers and those who simply watch the birds in the garden. If we're being honest, the world is a better place for their existence.

And the continued existence of this species looks to be assured today, for among the immaculate adults, at least ten of the next generation are feeding alongside them. They are a doddle to separate from the adults, in that they lack any of the bold red, white and black stripes on the face that renders their species normally so very unmistakable. Instead, the faces are blank and pale and dry-thistle coloured, with the dark eye giving them a little-bird-lost expression. If they didn't have the signature boldly patterned wing-bars they might just be quite tricky birds to identify.

August is a good time to see young goldfinches, because they come out in bulk at this time of the year, more so than earlier on – a month and a half later, for example, than young blue tits or starlings. This, of course, is a result of their diet – not just as fledglings, but in the nest as well. In contrast to most small birds, such as robins, chaffinches or wagtails, adult goldfinches feed their nestlings mainly on seeds, as opposed to insects, and deliver the seeds as a paste, mouth to mouth. Not surprisingly, breeding is easiest in the summer when the seeds of their main food plants, such as thistles and burdocks, as well as knapweeds, are ripening. Hence all-age goldfinch flocks are one of the features of summer.

And judging by the delight they are bringing here at The Patch – to birders, to dog-walkers, to the occasional hiker, even to the odd angler who drops his veneer of single-mindedness – let's hope it continues always to be so.

Tuesday 25 August 2009

It's a little-known fact that the warm sunshine of summer doesn't just brown the skin; it browns the local ducks as well. Or at least, it seems to. If you have never noticed this, and it happens to be the right time of year as you're reading, go and check out your nearest duck pond and see whether you can spot a brilliantly coloured specimen – or even a male duck, for that matter. You might just make out a black-and-whitish tufted duck, but I suspect that you will get stuck even on finding a decent mallard.

The Patch today has received a small influx of summer ducks: twenty mallards, two teals, a gadwall and a wigeon. And not one of them seems to be sporting male plumage. Indeed, on close inspection they all look similar, with only size and shape separating them: the diminutive teals, the small-billed wigeon, and the gadwall with its smooth crown. They are all mooching around in a small flock in one corner of The Lake, some on dry land, acting furtively, as if embarrassed by their appearance. They seem to be spending a great deal of time sleeping.

So what is the cause of this browning of British ducks? As in many of the happenings of August it has to do with the moult, but this one is a moult like no other. The changing of feathers in ducks also triggers a curious blurring of the sexes, at least from the outside. It is the month when the males dress like the females.

As you might have noticed from time to time, ducks taste very good indeed, and this fact is not lost on a wide range of predators in the wild. Anything that makes ducks minutely less than superior escapers with razor-sharp reactions and turbo-powered flight is going to render them vulnerable. And that is where the moult becomes problematical. They must moult once a year; they cannot avoid this any more than you or I, if we are wise, can avoid a visit to the dentist – it renews the feathers and keeps the plumage healthy. But moulting can slow a bird down. Perhaps for this reason, ducks find it expedient to moult all their flight feathers simultaneously, dramatically reducing the amount of time it would normally take to replace their wing plumage (most birds moult one or two primary feathers at a time, the same feather on each wing). It's a fair strategy and means that they are in top flying condition for most of the year.

In late summer, however, for a couple of weeks while they complete their accelerated moults, ducks are – well, almost sitting ducks, close to flightless, and needing to keep as low a profile as possible. Thus, the ducks on The Patch are keeping to their corner and not daring even to quack. But moulting also means that the usually conspicuous males are transformed. They dispense with their male plumage before they moult the flight feathers, and while most vulnerable they grow an undercover coat, known as 'eclipse plumage', to help them blend in with their surroundings. The emergency dress is very similar to that of the females.

The eclipse plumage renders ducks hard to identify, but there is at least one feature that a male can keep – bill colouration. Thus, I can tell the male mallards by their yellow bill and the male gadwall by its coal-black bill, both in contrast to the orange and brown bills of their females. The case of the wigeon is a little different, because although its bill is the same colour as that of the female, it retains the large white patch on the forewing that is a good distinction for the rest of the year. Probably it is expedient to keep just a little bit of male identity.

By the end of summer, with wings restored, the males moult yet again, this time into their resplendent masculine best. Once again the sexes are completely and excitingly different, and the gender distinction is marked by a strong upsurge in courtship, even nine months before breeding can actually begin. It is hard to avoid the conclusion, with all this exuberant display going on, that the ducks are relieved, as well as refreshed.

Great Wildlife Days

Saturday 26 August 2006

This was a day when one could smell autumn in the air. Early morning sunshine was enough to bake The South

Side, so that the late summer smells were wafting in the soothing breeze as if an oven door had been opened somewhere. The grass was gently simmering into hay and the leaves of the oak and hawthorn trees were turning crisp and slightly brown, giving off the scent of tannin. It was also a day when one could *see* autumn in the air. Every cubic metre of the outside world seemed to be replete with wind-borne pollen, mixed up with a multitude of insects living out short lives in eddy-swirled style. The thistles were spewing their white down out from their purple blossoms, like ranks of miniature smoking chimneys.

Best of all, though, it was a day when one could *hear* autumn in the air. An unseen greenshank called its triple-note 'tu-tu-tu' as it flew high overhead, a party of twenty adult swallows twittered conversationally on the move like hobbyist runners, and a party of four yellow wagtails drew attention to themselves as they headed south by calling a loud 'sweep'.

On such days as this, with clear skies and settled conditions, it is worth checking the bushes for migrants that have arrived overnight, but really a weather front is needed to bring them down in any numbers. Nevertheless, a spotted flycatcher appeared in Emily's Wood, sallying into the invertebrate gas, snapping up a meal every time and building itself up for the next leg of its journey. In the hawthorn hedge close to Old Ash bend, a common whitethroat worked the sunlit snags, while a reed warbler, taking a break from the monotony of its reed-bed habitat, sought sustenance in the shadowy interior. And from many a bush, the odd 'swilp' gave away the presence of juvenile chiffchaffs, the migrant birds that pass southern England in such abundance that, even when there's nothing else around, there's always the odd chiff.

On days like this it's not necessary to see too many birds to be satisfied. This is the time of year, the intoxicatingly delicious beginning to the autumn season, when one day might be slow, but there will be something interesting to see tomorrow, or if not, the next day. The autumn migration, in contrast to the spring one, is a drawn-out affair that delivers delights day after day, week after week. For any birder who isn't in a hurry, and particularly for a patch-birder, all that is required is metaphorically to settle back and enjoy it.

Thus it would have been easy enough just to get caught up in the autumnal spell and ride with it into a gentle stupor. Several good birds over a short space of time have the effect of a good meal: pleasant to take in, followed by a period of contented digestion. But today The Patch had other ideas – a jolt out of the blue, or perhaps the ultimate killer dessert. Beside Old Ash Bend, where The River turns south and a reed-bed (The Marsh) flanks its broadest reaches, my attention was caught by a sudden commotion among the mallards, which had hitherto been slumbering in the shallow water. They all lifted their heads in unison, jumped into the water and swam at considerable speed downriver.

Curiosity aroused, I scanned the open water – nothing. That was odd; clearly something had spooked the ducks, which are not given (unlike some birds, such as lapwings) to overreaction. However, after a couple of minutes I spotted a large blob in the water, on the edge of The Marsh. A quick scan of the binoculars revealed a dark brown, rounded head, and almost immediately the blob dived, in such a distinctive way that its identity was clearly revealed. It seemed to roll over into the water, going down head first and tail last, in the same way that one of the great whales rolls down into a dive. It was an otter. I kept scanning and, fifty metres upriver, that same rounded head appeared, before immediately submerging again and being lost to view.

I had heard rumours about otters in the waters of The Patch, but most of these had come from reports that were several years old. This particular sighting was, therefore, not just stunning – it had occurred at 9 a.m. on a Saturday, with the usual cars raging past on The 'A' Road, and with the world already wide awake – but was also confirmation that this charismatic mammal was indeed in the area.

The sighting was quick, but deeply satisfying and significant, too. The presence of otters confers a definite status on an area. Were The Patch ever threatened with development (which is pretty unlikely, admittedly), then the presence of this rare mammal would help to buttress the resistance against it. An otter-hosting patch also gains repute among local people, who know what a treasure and rare delight this mammal is, and think higher of their local countryside. Such people may think a wigeon is simply a pigeon spelt wrong, but their influence can be significant when decisions are made about an area.

These days otters are not as rare as they used to be. In the 1970s and 1980s they became almost extinct in southern England, but since that time they have made a remarkable recovery, returning to many of the rivers and wetlands that once provided homes and holts. It's good to see that this trend has even affected the waters of The Patch, too, the fragment of southern England that means so much to me.

SEPTEMBER

Thursday 3 September 2009

Not many birding highlights begin when you are about to enjoy a long soak in the bath. It was 7.30 p.m. when the phone rang. The light was fading and the children were in bed, and the prospect of a long winding-down evening loomed appealing and sweet. I thought twice about answering it.

But the voice on the other end said: 'I've got a phalarope. You'd better get down here quickly.'

It was Chris Parnell, and he had just run into the best bird ever recorded at our Patch.

I have not seen too many phalaropes in this country, let alone locally. And up until then, I had never seen one in the dark, either. By the time I had togged up for birding and parked the car along The Lane, the street lights on The 'A' Road were on and shining brightly.

But Chris, bless him, had remained stationed on the spot and I got to him before the wildfowl on The Lake became nothing more than shapes. He pointed, and panic stations were over. Phalaropes have a helpful habit of being tame, and this individual was swimming no more than five metres from where we were standing. This grey phalarope should have been out to the west in the Atlantic Ocean. Instead it was on a freshwater lake in early September, surrounded by coots, tufted ducks and two feverishly happy admirers.

Phalaropes, for those who don't know much about them, are captivating little birds. They are related to waders, such as curlews and plovers, the sort of birds you can see scampering over mud in estuaries and on the seashore, but have a very different lifestyle from the rest of their kin. Instead of wading, they spend most of their time swimming, rather like miniature ducks. And instead of spending the non-breeding season on mudflats, they head out into the world's oceans (the Atlantic for the grey phalarope and the Arabian Sea for the red-necked phalarope) and feed on plankton. To cope with this unusual diet, phalaropes have needle-like bills, and use capillary action to 'suck' small creatures into their mouths. They also have an odd and very endearing habit of routinely spinning around, as if they are about to be sucked down an imaginary sink, and this is supposed to stir up plankton, or in the breeding season insects and their larvae, so that the birds can feed in one spot.

Another quirk of phalarope behaviour is a breeding system known as role reversal. The title refers to the duties performed by the male and female, many of which switch over from the norm expected for avian kind. Thus, while in most bird species it is the female that incubates the eggs she has laid and looks after the chicks, in the case of the phalaropes it is the male. Furthermore, while in most species of birds the male takes the initiative in courtship and takes on an aggressive and assertive persona, this role falls to phalarope females. It is they who are larger and more colourful, it is they who may well reserve the right to form a pairing with more than one mate, and it is they who, when their duties are done, will migrate away from the breeding areas and take an indulgent post-breeding sabbatical. Meanwhile the males are saddled with much duller colouration, almost complete neglect and the wearing of the metaphorical pinafore.

Chris and I met at dawn the next morning, very much hoping

that the grey phalarope had spent the night at The Patch. It had done, and we found it in exactly the same place, swimming in circles, buoyant as polystyrene. We were able to get much better views in the brightening light, and some photographs, too. From the large grey patches on its back, intermixed with black wing-feathers, together with a thick bill and a curious suffusion of salmon-pink on its neck, we aged the bird as a juvenile grey phalarope moulting into the so-called first winter plumage that it would bear for that first, ocean-going winter of its life.

Our delight at spotting the phalarope was mixed with quite a degree of bewilderment as to what circumstances had contrived to bring it to our inland site. It's not that grey phalaropes don't turn up in strange places – they frequently do. But usually this happens during severe autumn storms, when south-westerly gales strike in October and November. Our bird was unusually early, and although it had been windy, it hadn't really qualified as phalarope weather.

The bird probably came from Svalbard, an archipelago between the North Pole and Norway's North Cape, where grey phalaropes are fairly numerous; or possibly from Iceland, where they are much rarer. Canada would seem a more distant prospect. Either way, it was on a long journey, and a long way off course.

The phalarope must have sensed just that. Within twenty minutes of first light, it flew off on strong, very rapid wing-beats, and never returned.

Great Wildlife Days

Sunday 10 September 2006

It's an unfortunate truth that all people, even if they are the keenest wildlife-watchers, have at heart a fractious relationship with wild creatures. Or maybe it should be stated another way: most wildlife has a fractious relationship with people, regardless of those individuals' tendencies and intentions. Even on the most innocent and gentle of strolls around The Patch, I am always certain to disturb as many birds as I see, even when I wish that I did not do so. And doubtless the four-footed animals – the badgers and mice and deer, always give me the widest berth possible.

That is why it is such a privilege, and a rare delight, to witness a snippet of wildlife behaviour occasionally that is private and raw and unsullied by one's presence. Wildlife cameramen and women manage to do this for much of their professional lives, usually by dint of hours of patient application within the confines of a hide, but for a normal patch-watching birder, such cameos of reality wildlife are a rarity.

Today, though, I was birding beside The Thicket looking for migrant warblers when my eyes were drawn to a dog fox a short distance away, on the farmer's field close to The Hedge that marks the north-western boundary of The Patch. There was plenty of thick long grass here, and the fox was looking down rather than up. Normally, foxes can be expected to be aware of humans instantaneously, but this one seemed so utterly absorbed that it could have been reading a novel in a library.

It was soon obvious what it was doing. Its concentration paid off as it detected some food in the long grass. Its body stiffened, except for a slight twitch of the ears. Then, after a slight backward sway, it sprung upwards using a kick of its back legs and landed in an elegant two-footed pounce, front paws together. This manoeuvre evidently trapped its prey to the ground, so the fox lunged down and took the unfortunate crea-ture in its jaws. It stood up again, and the prey, which looked like a field vole, hung limply until being swallowed in one go.

I expected this to be the end of the hunting show, but remark-ably the fox, still utterly single-minded and daring, just stood its ground. Within minutes it had made another leap, missing its quarry this time. The rich grassland was such a lure, such a complete haven of feeding possibilities, that it had time to leap again and catch another vole before, with something of a jolt (or perhaps a small clue in the wind), it came to its senses and looked around, as every fox always must. It soon became aware of me.

Or did it? To my astonishment, it turned its back and concentrated once more on the grass below, presumably beguiled by the delicious scent of another vole. For the fourth time it made a leap, as high and impressive as any before, but came to ground holding nothing more than grass roots and dirt. Apparently disgusted, it finally loped off and disappeared into the hedgerow.

Completely elated, I felt like clapping, for I had never seen a fox hunting in this way. But I didn't clap. Clapping is for public events, but this was eavesdropping, glancing through a window on a private moment.

Great Birding Days

Tuesday 14 September 2004

There cannot be a patch-watcher in the whole country who hasn't reminisced from time to time about the most memorable days on their favourite site. In fact, if you are a patch-watcher on an inland locality, where many days can be pretty slow and boring, you probably do this quite often. In fact, you probably have a league table, compiled over the years, to help you keep going in lean times. But then, how about going further, actually nominating the best of the best? In all the trips you have made over the years, in different conditions, with different motivations and seeing things that were memorable for completely different reasons, could you name the very best day you have ever had? I know I can: one day, for me, stands head and shoulders above all the rest.

The blessed day was 14 September 2004. It was a balmy autumn day, with weak sunshine but not much wind. It was early on in my acquaintance with my Patch, and I had yet even to taste the delights of The South Side, still very much out of bounds at the time. To tell the truth, much as I enjoyed watching over The Lake and The Thicket of my new stamping ground, I might not yet have been wholeheartedly devoted to a life of monitoring the comings and goings of birds here. There was much going on in my life at the time, and thrashing around a filled-in gravel pit for the occasional wader and warbler had not yet risen high among my priorities.

Perhaps 14 September changed all that. It is hard to say whether it did, at least on its own. But what I can say for certain is that it changed my opinion of The Patch and its merits, and persuaded me for the first time that it really could deliver some seriously good birds. My enthusiasm grew considerably from this time on.

And yet the wondrous thing is that it was hardly much of a visit. I probably didn't stay for more than about forty-five minutes – remember, I was extremely busy and distracted at the time. I also had a high-maintenance companion with me. Forty-five minutes, though, to change a life? It really did.

In those days there was hardly any disturbance at The Lake at all. Fishing hadn't yet begun; there was no Visitor Centre; even dog-walkers were quite a rarity. As a result it had just recently become a magnet for birds, and this now included a number that clearly saw it as a safe and quiet place to moult. The highlight was a black-necked grebe, a classy bird at any location, which was giving incredibly close views, down to its red eye and the cute upward curvature of its bill. It was ably supported by a small and quite deliciously mixed flock of ducks: mallards, four wigeons, a single shoveler, and the first gadwalls ever to touch down on the water – two males in eclipse plumage that had appeared a couple of weeks earlier. Amazingly, another unusual duck, a garganey, was also a member of this flock, and would allow enough of an approach to show off its signature stripy head and long body (which distinguishes it from the very similar teal, still a year off being recorded for the first time on The Patch), although it often hid itself in a quiet bay. I notched up every one of these species within a few minutes of sunlit watching.

Could this get any better? I checked through the flock of ducks to make sure I hadn't missed anything, and conveniently the moulting members all left the shore on which they were slumbering and swam across The Lake in single file, as if they were part of an identity parade – which, in a way, they were. Yes, it could get better. A decent look revealed a long-necked duck with pale plumage, a bluish bill and a blank expression on its face: a pintail, new for the site, the fourth such novelty of the month.

Black-necked grebe, garganey, pintail. This really was good stuff. And what was this shape appearing over the eastern horizon? Something big, long-winged and predatory-looking. Oh, surely not, it could not be...

It was, and for the next few moments my binoculars tracked an osprey as it plied south-west. It didn't stop at The Lake, but it had a good look as it flew fifty metres up in the warm September air. Maybe another day...

By now my hands were aching and I simply had to put my companion down. Up until now I had been holding him while trying to use the binoculars at the same time. It was a good job for me that the ducks and grebe had hitherto been close enough to observe easily, or I would have had to relinquish my hold earlier, and 2-month-old Samuel would probably not have enjoyed spending too long on the grass beside The Lake.

Osprey, black-necked grebe, garganey, pintail: what a cast list it had been for the very first birdwatching trip in my newborn son's entire life.

It was a big day, for both of us.

Wednesday 16 September 2009

It's the middle of the month that forms the middle of the migration season. Almost every bush and hedgerow in Britain should now be providing hospitality to transient birds for at least a moment of every day. Those hedgerows, which for most of the early part of the year provided roost sites and nesting sites, safe havens for shelter, are now mainly in the hotel business.

The Patch isn't alive with birds today, but some patient searching manages to tease out some of these transients. The bushes along the north-eastern edge of The Lake, only planted six or seven years ago, are now thick and luxuriant and provide ideal feeding areas for warblers, including reed warblers, which visit from the nearby lake-side reeds. A delicious mixture of hawthorn, bramble, wild rose and elder has made this part of The Patch the main hotel buffet.

My first warbler of the day is actually a sedge warbler, its commitment to the safe option of staying hidden undermined by an unquenchable curiosity. After I first glimpse it slipping out of sight, it cannot help itself, popping into view to look at me after a brief skulk in the depths of the foliage, and giving out a short scold that would presumably be unprintable upon translation. This individual might not be pleased to see me, but sedge warblers are always a delight, with their bold, pale eyebrows giving them a slightly surprised expression. The dark stripes on the pale brown back, and a bright chestnut rump, make them a highly superior small brown bird.

This sedge warbler, searching hard for insects on the sun-kissed, red-turning hawthorn leaves, obviously hasn't read its migration manual. What sedge warblers are *meant* to do at this time of year is to concentrate more or less exclusively on eating an insect called the plum-reed aphid, which, as its name suggests, is found in reed-beds. The aphids, which themselves migrate from blackthorn bushes and plum trees to reeds during the summer, evidently contain within their bodies some kind of super-ingredient that makes the warblers fat and hyper-fit and enables them to manage incredible flights. Sedge warblers fed on an aphid diet are thought to double their weight in a few short weeks, so they are fuelled like little jumbo jets. Then one evening they take off and fly for seventy or more hours non-stop, day and night, until they land in another country and another climatic zone.

It's an extraordinary feat unmatched by our other warblers, which take their migration in more leisurely fashion, in short steps, and the burst seems to be fuelled by this particular warbler's odd diet. Thus sedge warblers from throughout the country converge on reed swamp in southern England and northern France, where these insects are most abundant (there can be thousands on a single reed stem), and gorge themselves on this specialist diet until they are so primed for flight that they can make the transfer from Britain to western Africa in a single hop.

Still, notwithstanding the feats of its conspecifics, this sedge warbler is having none of this plum-reed nonsense. It is happy to munch on what it can glean from the foliage, and take its time.

The same bush hosts another warbler, the chiffchaff, which shows itself well among the rose hips and hawthorn berries. This bird isn't undone by its curiosity, like the sedge warbler, but by its fidgety nature, which means that it is never still. If ever a bird has a short attention span, it's the chiffchaff. It never remains for long on a single perch, but instead will flutter from one to another without evidently having much time to forage properly. It also frequently launches on short sallies to pick up a flying insect, and even when in one place simply cannot allow three seconds to pass without wagging its tail. This wag, which is apparently a slight side-flick, seems to have no obvious purpose, except to satisfy a restless nature. Chiffchaffs also flick their wings, and give an incessant 'swilp' call, and generally live three lives in the space of one.

This lively, blue-tit-sized chiffchaff, also endowed with pale eyebrows, but otherwise clad in the understated olive-green of summer-dried grass, has a similar destination to the sedge warbler. By November both birds, here sharing the same hawthorn, could be doing exactly the same thing 4,000 kilometres from here, on a tropical bush or reed-bed in the sun-drenched country of Senegal.

A loud and somewhat testy 'tak' call emanates from another

bush a few metres to the left, and I have bagged my third species of warbler. It is as yet unseen, but this retiring species, too, has its weakness. This time I simply have to place the binoculars on a patch of hanging dark berries, and the blackcap will come into view sooner or later: the fox may have its grapes, but the blackcap has its elders. Sure enough, it isn't long before the grey-brown forager emerges from the shadows and begins to pluck from the elder bunches, pulling each fruit off the stalk with its strong bill and swallowing it in a single gulp, consuming this food without any sense of relish, as if it were an addict. Within a few minutes it gulps seven or eight more. Blackcaps – and this is a male with its smart black skull-cap – give the impression of being thoroughly grumpy birds. They freely attack other species of small foraging berry-eaters, and punch above their weight.

Its considerable consumption might suggest that the blackcap is preparing for its own marathon flight, but in fact, this isn't so. Of all the warblers that can be found hereabouts, it has much the easiest autumn migration. It can harvest the berries for many weeks yet, and when it feels like it, can make the short hop to Spain or north-western Africa to spend the winter. Studies have shown that, on average, berries taken by birds in the Mediterranean are smaller than those of their counterparts further north, because the berry-bearing plant species are adapted to feed warbler mouths, which are in the majority there, rather than thrush mouths, which dominate here. So the blackcaps will have berries on tap, and will doubtless flourish.

The warbler list is coming on, but strangely they are all singletons today. In my half-hour visit I see single sedge warbler, chiffchaff and blackcap and then add in a reed warbler, a brown bird with such an extended bill and forehead that it gives a peculiarly long-nosed impression, and then a delightful, chestnut-winged common whitethroat, an individual sheepishly trying to share elderberries with the blackcap. It gives up and tries the blackberries instead; the hassle is too great.

I am keen to find the joker in the migratory warbler pack, the species that defies convention and logic to follow a very different path from the rest. It takes a little while, and necessitates a move down towards The Thicket where the bushes are thinner, but eventually a lesser whitethroat interrupts its secretive foraging and perches on top of a bramble for a short moment. There could scarcely be a neater warbler than this, with its washing-powder white underparts, dark brown upperparts and dark grey head; and this bird, like many, has a blackish mask around the eyes. There is nothing in its feeding ecology to suggest any diversion of behaviour from the other warblers I have seen today, yet this species, feeding on the same insects in the same bushes at the same height, and with the same aversion to disturbance, will fly south-east from here, and not south-west. At first it will travel to northern Italy, and then perhaps on to the Aegean or even the Holy Land, before dropping down into Africa and wintering as far south as Sudan or Ethiopia. So, while it is currently separated from its peers by perhaps fifty metres (and that incidentally), in three months that divergence will be closer to 5,000 kilometres, or a hundred thousand times as much.

Oh, the marvel of bird migration! Six closely related species in a row and every one with a different strategy to follow or a different destination to reach. All they have in common is the berries on my Patch, which provide a universal food for their astounding feats. By Christmas these individuals will together have travelled more than 20,000 kilometres. And, who knows? Perhaps I will see them back again next year.

Tuesday 22 September 2009

A cross in the bird log indicates that today was the day that I saw my last house martins of 2009. The first were a couple on 6 April, so their summer has spanned just less than six months. Compare this with previous years: my earliest ever have been on 31 March and my latest on 13 October.

Swallows are customarily later in departing; passage continues in dribs and drabs until at least the third week of October.

I have never before recorded the last house martin of The Patch year in September, let alone three-quarters through the month. In fact, this petering out is more than two weeks earlier than average. It's symptomatic of what has been a very bad year for these insectivores. The weather has been appalling, the nests on the waterworks failed, and the bird is suffering a severe decline in Britain. This is a common bird that we need to keep monitoring.

Although it's common, the house martin is also an extraordinarily mysterious bird. When it departs Britain and Europe in autumn, it certainly goes to Africa, but nobody yet knows where the real concentrations are. About 300,000 individuals have been ringed in Britain, but only a single bird has been found south of the Sahara. And despite the fact that up to 90 million birds cross into Africa from Europe every year, they are hardly ever seen anywhere even in the vastness of that continent. There have been large flocks seen in places as wide apart as Nigeria and South Africa, but only in the tens of thousands, and certainly not millions. The truth is, remarkable though it may seem, that most of the millions of house martins disappear into thin air.

Another astonishing mystery surrounding the house martin is where it goes to bed at night. Not when it's breeding; it sleeps in the nest at that time. The mystery concerns where birds sleep when they are on their migratory journeys (as well as in Africa, of course). Swallows and sand martins gather together, sometimes in very large concentrations, in reed-beds, and they can be a spectacular sight and sound. But house martins don't join such concentrations. In fact, nobody sees them in numbers at roost, any more than anyone sees them at large in Africa.

Of all the birds that disappear in autumn, none goes into such a fog of mystery as the humble house martin.

OCTOBER

Great Birding Days

Wednesday 3 October 2007

It looks and feels like October today. There was a hint of frost last night, a good clue that September is over. But for a birder, that's life. The two months vie to be the most exciting of the year for birdwatching, especially since both are heavy with migratory movements. Throughout these months birds are on the move in their millions, or hundreds of millions. It's as if somebody lights a fuse and almost every bird explodes away from wherever it has been breeding, and is thrust into a migratory swirl lasting for weeks. The debris can settle almost anywhere, even The Patch.

There are some days in birding when one can just smell that something good is around. The bushes are just a little more active than usual, and there is often a crisp feel to the air. But really it is just a birder's gut instinct. Today is such a day, though, and I feel a definite tinge of expectancy. The Patch's bushes are laden with berries, and perhaps this is what fuels the anticipation. The feast is laid and the guests have been invited. Will they turn up?

When I first visited The Patch in 2002 there weren't too

many berries on display, just those produced by an old hedge along the unmade track along the northern perimeter, and some next to The Thicket. Since then the Water Company has planted two sides of The Lake with a splendid array of native berry-bearing bushes, including blackthorns, elders, hawthorns and guelder rose, and they have now matured into a restaurant for hungry birds. Already blackbirds and warblers have taken up the offer. Very soon the winter thrushes, redwings and field-fares, will have their turn. But what is it today?

Within a few minutes I have an answer, when a thrush-sized bird appears on top of a bramble next to The Thicket. It is extremely furtive, and keeps its head down, trying to keep out of sight. But I can still see that there is the hint of a pale band around the chest and that, most significantly, it has pale edges to its flight feathers. It is a ring ouzel, a great rarity here, only the second record. Within seconds it has dived down into the depths of the thick vegetation, and I know from experience of this shy bird that I won't see it again. But at least it gives a confirmatory 'tack' call to say goodbye.

There is something extra special about hosting a ring ouzel on The Patch, because of the delicious disparity about where it breeds and where it travels. These blackbird-like thrushes are found in hilly areas, usually above 250 metres, often in climates with driving wind and rain. They like a territory with a river, some close-cropped grass and a few bushes, where they live a life of secrecy. Here at The Patch there is nothing that would suit breeding ring ouzels. But today they have left the mountains and have touched down in this very ordinary place, a stopover on their short migration to the mountains of North Africa.

There are blackbirds and song thrushes sharing these hedges today, and both species will spend a great deal of time over the next few months gorging themselves on nothing but berries. They must appreciate the berry season – which only goes to show how well the plants are manipulating them. Berries, with their bright colours or ultraviolet reflectance, together with their high energy package, are designed specially to attract birds. The idea is that the bird eats the berry, but the seed inside is too hard to be digested and is therefore ejected with the faeces. The bird, therefore, is 'used' by the plant as an agent of dispersal.

Is the plant really using the bird? Excellent evidence comes from southern Europe, where birds also eat a lot of berries, in Spain and Portugal for example. The key is that, where larger birds such as thrushes and starlings are the principle berry-eaters in Britain, having migrated down from northern and central Europe, in southern Europe the major berry-eating family is the warbler family, which contains very small species, most of them dwarfed by a great tit. And the berries? Scientists have shown that the average size of a berry in southern Europe is a great deal smaller than in Britain. In other words, the commodity appears to fit the market.

And have you ever wondered why the principal berry season is in the autumn, as opposed to the summer or the spring? It's again because of the market. In the autumn there are more birds around than at almost any other time of year (adults and the surviving juveniles) and, significantly, they are very much on the move. In the world of the berry, high numbers plus high volumes of movement makes for efficient dispersal.

The ring ouzel isn't bothered. It's quite content to be manipulated if it means a full stomach.

Monday 19 October 2009

I went out today to do my usual count of the wildfowl of The Patch. There were plenty of birds about and it was absorbing. The results weren't especially startling (fourteen gadwalls, twenty wigeons, thirty tufted ducks), but at least one day they can be compared to future Octobers, and scientists might make use of the figures. But I have to admit to you that, during the process of looking at coots and going 'one, two, three…', another count became rather insidiously intriguing. It was the number of species present. The trouble is, whenever I have a good day seeing a good variety of birds, I just cannot stop myself making lists. And when the figure gets good, the result is always the same. I neglect the proper count and try to beat my Patch day-record.

Patch day-records are about the most trivial and useless counts one could ever do. If there are fourteen gadwalls at a place and time and in certain conditions, that means something. But if on a day I see fifty species, it means absolutely nothing except that one birdwatcher saw fifty species in one place on one day. Keeping these day-records is about as anorak as things can get. I am embarrassed that I ever try – no matter that I actually try quite often! I cannot justify it. What good is it to anyone to know that a stock dove flew over and lifted the total by one? Absolutely none.

But if you are a patch-watcher, you already like making lists, don't you? Yes, you count ducks and roosting finches and gulls, and you monitor breeding birds. But you simply love your overall all-time patch-list, don't you (mine's 142 species, by the way), and you cannot resist finding new ones. And there's no doubt that one day you thought: 'Wow, there were a lot of species about today', and you counted them up, and raised your eyebrows – and lo, your patch day-record was born. No doubt you never actually planned to try to beat it, but on another day some time later you thought, 'That was a special day', and you sat down to count up and realized that the number was very close to the previous one. And if you like lists, you may have dragged yourself out for another hour, just to see some ludicrous bird like a pheasant or a grey wagtail, and managed to break it by one species. Doubtless you felt ashamed at such a trivial visit, but you treasured it anyway in the guilty part of your mind.

Well, one cracking August day a few years ago I managed, in several hours' birding, to see sixty-four species on The Patch. That is pretty damn good for such a small site well inland. In fact, it was so good that it very nearly made the trivial act of listing on this day respectable; if it had been higher, up to seventy or even eighty, it would even have been remarkable, and then I might not even have been embarrassed about attempting it – I could have told other birders and they would definitely have been impressed. As it turned out, though, this day-list was so pretty damn good that it became glued in, and has maintained its position at the top ever since. In fact, it has become a millstone around my neck. All attempts to break it have come to naught.

But today is looking very good. All the waterfowl were in place during the count and several tricky-to-record species were good enough to make an appearance while it was going on: a peregrine flew over, for instance, a stonechat was along the causeway between The Lake and The Quarry and I heard a water rail calling from the stream on the edge of The Shire Field. By the end of the wildfowl log I returned home and counted up fifty-one species. In a single go, that was pretty hot.

The fifty-one species, I knew, excluded five or six that should be a doddle to find. I had simply missed several gulls, collared dove, rook and reed bunting, just by not looking for them. And because I had kept my eyes to the water, I had also missed several birds that should be easy enough to find in one of the woods. Whichever way I looked at it, the record was on. No matter that I shouldn't be wasting time today by chasing absurdly common birds that I have seen thousands of times before. No matter that there wasn't really anybody who I could tell of the record who might actually be interested. No matter that there were no rules and I could easily fabricate a list (and it wouldn't matter). My search for immortality (or not) was on.

A trip to The South Side was imperative. Guiltily, I left my work at home, cleaned the binocular lenses, and went sniffing for new birds. Another hour and the magic figure of sixty-five should be within reach. Or at least it had better be, because the light would begin to fade after that.

The South Side, it turned out, was in a mischievous mood. The woods teased with half-sightings of distant birds, and the grassland taunted with nothing. Twenty minutes into the hour, and I had seen a paltry two extra birds, a tree creeper and a jay, and it was clear that things were not going to plan. But the trouble with patch day-listing is that you can't just up and leave and try somewhere else, you've simply got to keep going exactly where you are. It's a good life lesson – carry on when things are not going for you... Aha! What was that calling from the depths of Samuel's Wood – yes, a nuthatch, feeding on the one beech tree in the whole wood. Another 'tick'.

And then a big surprise. Next to Samuel's Wood, The River flows in secret. The public aren't allowed in, and for several hundred metres there is wood on both sides and very little comes this way. It's a peaceful stretch that acts as something of a refuge for shy creatures (otters, kingfishers, crocodiles, a puma). At times it feels as wild as a branch of the Danube Delta. On approaching it this time I check the usual multi-branched dead tree that has partly fallen into The River from the near side. It looks exactly like the sort of perch that would be ideal for vultures, for example, but usually hosts cormorants and herons instead. But today there is something distinctly exotic there, and I am immediately stunned: a flock of no fewer than fourteen mandarin ducks, each draped on its branches like a colourful beach towel. The males are ludicrously patterned, featuring crazy markings of orange (the exact colour of mandarin oranges, as it happens). On the head there is an opulent fan of orange highlights drooping down from the cheeks, and on the back there are sails sticking up from the wing. With a purplish breast and a broad white band over the eyes, which turns into a plume, there is a strong argument to say that mandarin males are so overdressed that they look a little silly. However, one very good point about mandarins is that they never really behave like exotic ducks. They are splendidly timid and they fly very fast, the males making little whiplash sounds as they tear away and the females making a call that could be a very feminine blow of the nose. And indeed, true to form, the whole flock took off with such ceremony and vigour that they were verging on rude.

Nevertheless, the mandarin ducks were a revelation: new for the day, of course, but also new for the year, and even new for The Patch itself. Here a tick, there a tick, everywhere a tick, tick. Pure delight.

The mandarins should really have triggered a surge in sightings, but actually all I got was an afterglow. A couple more species showed, including the collared dove, rook and reed bunting, but the light soon began to fade and it became obvious that I had left the afternoon trip until too late in the day. But then again, if I had come out earlier, I would probably have missed the mandarins.

In the end I saw sixty-one species, which is still very good for any inland site, but not a record for The Patch. A couple of species found their names on a list all right, but only a black list, the names tarnished by the heinous crime of not allowing themselves to be seen; remarkably, they included both common and great black-backed gulls, which are usually common enough in October.

But no matter – the record stands. Next time I will concentrate on proper birding. And of course, you understand, I don't actually take day-lists seriously. Honestly, I don't.

Monday 26 October 2009

The Patch doesn't look familiar in the pre-dawn dark of October. The friendly woods and bushes of The South Side loom murky and sinister as I wander down to the banks of The River. Its water looks black enough to be a lava flow. It's not at all welcoming here in the gloom and for some reason I find myself trying to keep as silent as possible, perhaps instinctively afraid of attracting attention to myself in the darkness.

I'm here to watch the sky, though. And at the very same time, all over the country, other birdwatchers are doing exactly the same, waiting, bleary-eyed, for dawn to break. We have all made the pilgrimage to witness the lightening skies of late October unveiling a wondrous, but poorly known wildlife phenomenon. We are hoping to behold some visible migration.

Visible migration is almost an oxymoron. It is called visible because one can actually watch birds on the move, but when there isn't much light, and the skies are as grey as Welsh shale, all one tends to see is small shapes bustling over, usually in small flocks. It isn't usually very spectacular, and much of the joy is in the skill of listening and identifying the shapes.

It is true migration, though. On autumn mornings, certain birds find it expedient to make limited movements during the first three or four hours of light. Most of these birds are seed-eaters, or berry-eaters. On the whole the insectivorous migrants, such as flycatchers and warblers, begin their migration at dusk and travel for a few hours before setting down in complete darkness, and their migration is impossible to watch in the field. The morning migrants of late autumn, however, perform their journeys early on in the day, giving birders the privilege of watching them on the move.

Part of the excitement of the whole phenomenon is that one can only imagine where the birds have come from, and where they are going. I have stated that the movements are local, and this makes them easier to understand and appreciate than the vast intercontinental marathons completed by such birds as swallows and house martins. Thus a bird such as a chaffinch might only move from one part of the country to the other, perhaps covering no more than eighty or ninety kilometres in a morning. And for every morning there may be a different departure point and destination, depending on the wind direction, weather and season. This is visible migration, but that does not make it any less of a mystery.

Talking of mysteries, one that I am grappling with is why my Patch is pretty hopeless for visible migration. Today is by no means the first time I have tried to see a decent number of moving shapes. I always see something, but other birders locally post endless lists of delicious species passing over their patches, and these patches are often no more than a few kilometres from here. They see woodlarks, crossbills, tree pipits and so on; all of them dream birds for my Patch. But visible migration has always been hard work, and sometimes that doesn't feel very fair.

There are some logical arguments to explain the drawbacks regarding my Patch. For a truly respectable visible migration watch-point an elevated viewpoint is really necessary, be it a hill, a cliff or even a tall building – there's a building in the middle of London, Tower 42, from where people see all sorts of unlikely things. Another useful commodity is coastline, which is where the best visible migration is seen. My Patch, being inland and as flat as the tennis lawns at Wimbledon, just doesn't meet the right specifications. But that doesn't entirely explain why there seems to be so little overhead movement. We do, after all, have a river running alongside, and birds often follow landmarks such as rivers. And other sites nearby, with equally uninspiring credentials, do turn up decent birds.

Perhaps it is simply a matter of selecting the right patch of my Patch, or selecting the right wind, or the right weather? I think I have tried everything, but it could be a matter of stumbling upon perfect conditions. That's one of the joys of patch-watching – one actually has to make one's own discoveries.

Equally, I could be flogging a dead horse, or at least a moribund one. I might spend the next twenty years watching my hallowed skies and see nothing more than a few meadow pipits. Yet, as mentioned before, a patch is a patch, with its faults as well as its delights, and one day there will surely be a decent bird flying over here.

One day, yes. But could it be today? The early signs aren't very good. It's dark and birdless, and the light wind seems to be sighing in complaint at the very thought of starting the day. The traffic on the main road is at full flow, rendering any bird that does anything but shout all but inaudible. The sluggish light seems to be caught under its own clouds; it's the sort of day when the sun never seems to rise properly. And for a good half an hour, absolutely nothing happens.

Twenty or so yawns pass and then at last, something. It so happens that the first of the migrants is heard and not seen – an invisible visible migrant. But it's a redwing, a genuine bird on the move, not a local bird moving from one place to another. These birds have a sharp call, rather like a purse-lipped exhalation of pain, and I can track the progress of this individual overhead, ploughing into the south-westerly wind. Its call is followed by another one and, despite myself, I fall into delirious optimism. It is 7.40 a.m. This could signal a passage of birds.

The next few minutes are indeed delirious – or at least, delirious for here. The redwing's call was like a referee's whistle starting off a match, and suddenly different birds are moving this way and that. It must have been the slightest change in light intensity, which said 'go!' and they are on the move.

The two redwings are followed by another flock of twenty, also riding into the wind, moving fitfully with their trademark bursts of wing-beats followed by a hesitant glide. They keep closely together, as if wary of their surroundings. Not so a couple of skylarks – they fly independently, uttering their quiet 'chirrup' ripple of a call, a single bar out of their usual flight song. They are followed by a burst of finch species, each manoeuvring with a bounding flight that always looks carefree and slightly out of control. First a flock of goldfinches moves over, each small body seemingly tethered to the rest by invisible elastic, and first one and then another seems to break away from the flock, only to be reeled in again. Then longer-tailed, more elegant chaffinches move over, in a discrete party of three – these species are classic October visible migrants. Some visible migration watchers record hundreds a day, even thousands. But three will do for now.

Better still is to come. A familiar feeble, high-pitched, almost whining call heralds a fly-past by a small group of siskins. Attractive greenish finches with thin bills and streaked plumage, siskins are rare at The Patch, with just a handful of records a year. They need far more woodland than the relatively sparse offerings here, although there is a stand of alders that might attract a flock down occasionally to feast on the seeds. In the poor light these midgets are indistinguishable from the goldfinches. But calls are everything.

And could this be something special? It is only a single bird, and the call is faint. Yet there's no doubt. It's a redpoll. Where it came from I don't know, and its destination is similarly a mystery. It certainly isn't stopping. Yet this is my first redpoll on site for a long seven years; the first came on my first-ever visit to The Patch in 2002, when one was feeding on the side of the unfilled Lake. How this place has changed.

Other birds pass over in a mad period when The Patch, for the briefest of moments, becomes a migration highway: meadow pipits, wagtails, even a wandering mistle thrush. Sixty-seven birds come over in ten magical minutes, one every ten seconds. And several of them are scarce visitors here. I never got a decent view of a single one of them; they were nothing but calling shapes. The migration might have been barely visible, but the movement wasn't bad.

I will come this way again, to the point where The River dips south next to Emily's Wood. Perhaps this is that fabled hotspot where all visible migration dreams become a reality, and within weeks there will be hordes of rarities here. It seems pretty doubtful, but on my walk back to breakfast, the sky seems to be brightening fast.

Great Birding Days

Friday 27 October 2006

I went out birding on this crisp early morning, but it wasn't a bird that stole the show, it was a mammal. As I wandered down The Lane beside the northern shore of The Lake, a weasel scampered across my path, and then moved to one side of the track, keeping hidden in the vegetation. The only clue to its continued presence was the angry 'chink' call of a couple of blackbirds. For some minutes the anxious calls moved along with the predator, putting the hedgerow on high alert.

As ever, it wasn't much of a view of a weasel, just a glimpse of a brown, long-bodied animal on the run, loping with two-footed hops until it gained the safety of cover. Weasels always astonish by their diminutive size, which makes them look like elongated mice, or perhaps running sausages. Their tail is short and seems like an afterthought, quite dissimilar from the bushy and black-tipped tail of the weasel's close relative, the stoat. Yet despite their dimensions, weasels are formidable predators, and any glance at the head, flattened and cobra-like and with deadly teeth, gives me the creeps.

This was the first, and so far only, sighting I have ever made of a weasel at The Patch, and I have never seen a stoat here at all – although one of The Patch's regulars, Trevor Thorpe, a fine all-round naturalist, has done so twice (but hasn't seen a weasel). I suspect that between us we have probably made a thousand visits here, lasting an average of one hour, and this lack of sightings shows what elusive animals these elongated killing machines are. Yet both species are likely to be resident, because they are quite territorial, and there is plenty here in the way of food – rabbits for the stoat and voles for the weasel.

The sheer secrecy of their lives is impressive, especially since both are active both by day and night, and they don't shun areas with a large human population nearby. They just use their senses, keep their heads down and steer clear of people. The weasel spends a great deal of its time underground; being a specialist in voles, which live in burrows, this little assassin is so small and slim that it can follow its prey into the very sanctuary where a rodent might think it is safe. The weasel can smell the vole's presence, so there is no escape. It would seem that a vole simply has nowhere to hide.

Incidentally, if it isn't smell that gives a vole away, it would seem to be its urine. It is now well known that the vole wee, which is produced every few minutes and in relatively copious quantities, has a chemical component that is visible in the ultra-violet spectrum. Unfortunately, another of this rodent's predators, the kestrel, can spot the urine trails while it is flying or hovering over a site. Apparently the trails give the kestrel an idea of the abundance of voles in a particular location, and the raptor then knows over which fields it can concentrate its hunting.

Mammal trapping on The Patch, mainly in the area of The Quarry, has revealed a big population of field voles – it's amazing that there are any left – and the local pair of kestrels, who breed just off-site, can often be seen hovering over The West Fields. However, despite the abundance of rodents, I cannot ever remember seeing a free-running individual, even though voles, like weasels and stoats, are active during the day. I have caught bank voles and wood mice just across The 'A' Road in mammal traps, and there are plenty of yellow-necked mice locally, so these rodents probably live in Samuel's Wood, the richest broadleaf area on site. Yet, all these creatures are almost impossible to see.

Once again this demonstrates just how poorly we naturalists actually know our patches. Oh yes, we probably see a lot of what goes on among bird populations, but of secretive mammals we know hardly anything, and as for the various invertebrates, forget it. We could wander over an area for fifty years and get only the merest snapshot of what is going on in its hidden corners.

And a snapshot is precisely what I got today.

NOVEMBER

Monday 2 November 2009

On arrival at the shores of The Lake today I was met by a sight that would make an angler's blood freeze. Slithering around in the north-east corner was a whole mass of cormorants, making the water boil with their constant diving. There was such a confusion of bodies that they were difficult to count at first, but I eventually managed to log the princely number of sixty-two.

This is the highest number I have ever recorded at The Patch, yet I feel instinctively that it represents the future. The Lake is well stocked with fish, and with a very large body of water to be filled in within a few weeks, the site is going to become cormorant heaven. Aside from the abundant food, there are the tall pylons on which the birds can sit and dry their wings safely, and The River nearby where they can fish if The Lake happens to freeze over. Sixty-two birds is actually quite a modest number and within a few months I expect there to be many more.

This, of course, is all bad news for the anglers. It isn't such bad news as they always seem to think, but it certainly does raise the prospect of conflict and angst. The only saving grace is that cormorants are shy birds, and The Lake is small enough for them always to flush when they are disturbed. So at least when the anglers are present the cormorants, for the most part, will stay away.

The conflict between anglers and cormorants seems to be a classic clash between bird and man, between countryside and town and between two constituencies of hobbyists. The clash between bird and man is simple enough to appreciate: both are trying to catch fish. However, as far as I am aware, only the human side actually gets hot under the collar about it; the cormorants just serenely get into the water and do what nature intended in order to fill their bellies. The anglers, meanwhile, get extremely cross and spit out invective towards their more able fishing rivals. As far as I understand it, they resent the cormorants because they think that the birds deplete fish stocks, which is another way of saying that the birds are catching fish that, in the view of the rod and line enthusiasts, actually belong to them. Quite why the anglers feel they have the first rights in the wild to wild-living fish, at least along rivers and on the coast, is beyond my understanding: surely both man and bird are equally entitled to do their catching? Furthermore, the scientists seem, at present, to be stubbornly unable to prove that cormorants actually do deplete fish stocks anywhere where fish can come and go, concluding that the anglers, on the whole, are blaming the birds incorrectly in most areas, although not in closed systems such as fish farms and, indeed, lakes such as the one on The Patch. Looking at it as dispassionately as possible, the anglers are being a bunch of buffoons. What I also find quite risible is that the anglers will sometimes complain that the cormorants injure their precious fish, while apparently it is fine for them to lure those same fish with a hook that will then go through the fishes' mouths.

Of course, most anglers are decent folk who, I suspect, feel that they are on the downtrodden side of a culture clash. In recent years the countryside lobby has felt besieged both by government and the urbanized population. They feel that their opponents don't understand them and appreciate the depth of their soul-ties and general attachment to the countryside. Quite rightly, they feel that townies don't understand that the countryside is messy and bloodthirsty, not a sanitized haven of goodwill and peace. They instinctively appreciate that many relationships between man and animals are at heart abusive to the animals: after all, in the end, we kill and eat many of them. Hunting runs in their bloodlines, and the idea that cormorants should be shot at times is logical and natural.

Actually, once you understand the workings of the countryside, as opposed just to natural history, it is much easier to have sympathy with this opinion, even if you don't agree with it. And even the most ardent conservationist would have to admit that hunting of all kinds, including pheasant-shooting and foxhunting, has helped to preserve the countryside over the years and prevent Britain becoming suffocatingly urbanized.

But the countryside lobby is also its own worst enemy, because it isn't good at choosing its battles. For example, in 2009 fishery interests kicked up a stink about the planned re-introduction of European beavers to Scotland. These rodents are about the most harmless animals you could possibly introduce back into the British wild, and there is not a shred of evidence from anywhere in the world that beavers harm any fishery stocks, not even in sites where they have been put back after many years of absence. But the fisheries lobby complained anyway, because that's what they always do, and as a result they looked foolish and mean-spirited.

There is a danger that the same thing will happen over cormorants. All the studies suggest that, in open systems, cormorants don't cause fish stocks to decline. Self-evidently the piscivores can do so in closed systems, such as lakes and ponds, and especially at fish farms, so here there is a sensible argument to be made. But yet again, the anglers lobby for cormorants to be culled, when it would be far more sensible to take other measures, such as giving the fish places to hide. But by wanting blood and, in general, blaming cormorants for a lot of things for which they are not culpable, the anglers make themselves look foolish and reactionary. They need not do so.

This leads on to the third intriguing culture clash, between anglers and birdwatchers. Despite both constituencies being lovers of the countryside and lovers of wild animals, these two groups don't always get on very well, which is a pity, because if they joined forces more often they would have a powerful collective voice. But to me, this is largely the fault of those who carry rod and line. Their poorly controlled minority are usually the ones who stoke up enmity with birdwatchers and, quite frankly, some of them need to grow up a bit in their opinions about cormorants.

Anyway, as I muse on the maelstrom that their presence here causes, I am able to enjoy the cormorants' appropriately turbulent antics. At first it isn't obvious that there is anything other than chaos going on, like a sort of aquatic version of the opening of the January sales. But a closer look reveals that the birds are co-ordinating their dives; when one goes, most of the others around them go also. This is known to be intentional, because when all the birds dive down together, they cause panic among the fishes below, making them easier to catch. One can infer that there is a shoal around that corner of The Lake, where all the sixty-two cormorants reckon that they can catch a meal.

Cormorants live a curious life, divided between hugely aquatic and not aquatic at all. On the one hand they are supremely adapted for a life in the water: they are one of only a small number of birds that have all of their four toes webbed; their feet are set back so that they are powerful and fast swimmers; their bones are not as hollow as those of most other birds, so that their bodies are heavier and less buoyant than other birds; and their feathers are specially adapted to absorb water.

Cormorants also swallow stones to help them sink down easily, and presumably don't ever swallow too many.

Yet despite these extraordinary modifications, cormorants seem to spend remarkably little time actually in the water. Think of the occasions when you have seen them – it's probably when they are flying or simply loafing on a log or rock. A typical view of a cormorant isn't the arch-predator streaking through the water, but instead the large, awkward-looking, long-necked bird standing with wings outstretched in heraldic posture, the living washing line. The cormorant is so supremely efficient at catching prey that it can afford to spend much of its time doing nothing.

Incidentally, there is apparently more to this hanging out of the wings than simply drying them. Experiments on cormorants found that they will often keep their wings in when digesting warm fish, but hold them out when the fish they have eaten were cold. Evidently the outstretched posture also aids digestion.

Anyway, today has proved to be a good one for fishing birds at The Lake. Along with the cormorants there were also three grey herons around, which seek similar foods and, incidentally, don't seem to excite the same ire from anglers as their darker colleagues do, and there were a small number of great crested grebes around – the latter a truly full-time aquatic bird, incidentally.

Finally, along the new causeway between The Lake and The Quarry (soon to be The New Lake), I disturbed a small bird which caused my heart to skip with excitement and frustration for the fractional duration of the observation. As the waif flitted away with the typical fitful and somewhat feeble style typical of pipits, it gave off a call that instantly ruled out the usual common species here, the meadow pipit. The call was stronger and more confident – definitely either a rock or a water pipit, both new species for The Patch! Another half-call and I would have been able to tell which one, but the rare visitor had said enough and made for the opposite side of The Quarry, never to be seen again.

Both rock pipit and water pipit are likely visitors to an inland lake in November, and both have enticingly intriguing migratory patterns. The water pipit is the only bird that migrates off the mountains of central Europe to winter in Britain, moving in the improbable direction of north in autumn. The rock pipit's origin, however, is probably as a bird that has bred in northern Britain, perhaps Scotland. Either way, both species have had interesting paths to follow to The Patch.

Of these species, the rock pipit spends its time foraging along the shoreline and will, in addition to the usual invertebrates, snatch the occasional small fish in a rock-pool, making it one of the very few passerine birds to exploit this food source. In a day for piscivores, this one must qualify as the least likely of all to disturb the peace of The Patch's anglers.

Friday 6 November 2009

Early November marks the peak of one of the least understood of all major British birding events. It is nothing if not remarkable, and in view of its mysterious nature every birder might be expected to speak about it in excited and anticipatory tones in the weeks leading up to its zenith. Yet the astonishing truth is that many birdwatchers don't even realize that it happens and, if they do witness it in progress, they then don't realize that something special is going on.

I'm up early this morning to catch the phenomenon, standing near to The River's Old Ash Bend as the sun rises behind the partly defoliated poplar trees that flank Emily's Wood. The weather is clear overhead and there's a light southerly wind blowing, meaning that conditions are not too bad. Something should get going.

The first flock arrives only as I blow into my gloves for the tenth time to keep the fingers warm. A tight, well-disciplined mass appears silently overhead, some thirty metres or so above me, with perhaps two hundred birds in it, moving in very steady fashion to the south-west. They form one big oval and every single bird seems to keep the same personal space from the rest, so the flock keeps its shape as it moves across the sky. All the birds flap at the same speed, and no birds deviate in any way from the communal direction; the overall impression is that the birds are well-drilled to almost military precision.

The next birds to arrive are in smaller, more informal parties. Some contain just a handful of birds, others up to thirty or forty, but between them they make the overall total mount. Interestingly, these smaller flocks don't keep their shape like the big party, perhaps because with fewer individuals there aren't the same constraints to keep discipline. Anyway, after fifteen minutes I have seen almost four hundred birds. In typical visible migration style, there is then a pause before, as a finale, another group of a couple of hundred or so goes over, another flying oval to darken the sky. In the meagre half hour I have to spare this morning my total of birds is in excess of six hundred. Other birdwatchers locally record that the passage lasts until noon, so at a conservative estimate at least five thousand of these birds will have flown over The Patch this morning. And this is by no means an exceptional number.

So, what are these mystery migrants? I have deliberately avoided mentioning them until now, because if you are a typical birder you will not be a fan of them: they are woodpigeons. Typically, they excite nothing but apathy among everybody, whatever they do, yet the late October and early November movements of these birds can be truly special. Honestly, however much you don't appreciate a portly woodpigeon in your garden, it is hard not to be impressed by a really large group of hundreds moving over – they truly can darken the sky.

But there's a great deal that we don't understand about these movements, which can be huge – counts on the South Coast of

England sometimes reach 50,000 in a few hours. Well, actually, we don't understand anything at all. We don't know where the flocks come from and we don't know where they are going – which pretty much adds up to a bit of a blank.

You might think that all the techniques available for studying bird movements, including ringing and satellite tracking, might have sorted out the mystery by now. So far, though, results are just confusing. The median distance that ringed woodpigeons in Britain move between the time of their ringing and their recovery (as a corpse or a recapture) is only five kilometres, suggesting that they are extremely sedentary. Very few woodpigeons ringed in Britain have ever been recovered abroad, and equally very few foreign-ringed woodpigeons have ever been recovered in Britain. The statistics tell us that British woodpigeons are not great travellers.

But just this morning I can see that my six hundred or so woodpigeons all travelled more than five kilometres, for this was at least the span of the sky. The stream of woodpigeons flying determinedly at a significant height was definitely travelling somewhere, with a destination in mind. Some scientists dismiss the late autumn woodpigeon flocks as nothing more than local movements between roost sites and feeding sites, or between two different feeding sites. But, while some movements are undoubtedly of this nature, I cannot see how the really big movements can be explained like this, otherwise they would surely continue throughout the winter, which they don't. And besides, if tens of thousands of pigeons can be seen on the South Coast heading out to sea, then surely they are going to foreign soil?

Just to add to the confusion, there have been several observations of very large flocks of woodpigeons flying out to sea and towards France, only to return to our shores after what could almost be described as a day-trip. What on earth are these birds doing? It simply compounds the puzzle.

And puzzling, of course, is how we patch-watching birders

like things to be. There is something sweet about routine observations confounding the researchers, and something still sweeter about watching a mystery unfold in one's backyard. And when a mystery concerns one of the commonest and most unpopular birds in Britain, it simply exemplifies the delicious teasing of us by the impenetrably complex natural world.

Talking of mysteries, I had an unexpected insight today into the life history of another remarkable British creature, the common eel. It was unexpected because, after the woodpigeon vigil I walked past a man whom I didn't recognize in Emily's Wood, and immediately felt slightly suspicious. This part of The Patch is not accessible to the public, and the site occasionally plays host to poachers and other ne'er-do-wells (the anglers talk about them all the time). It turned out that the other man decided that I was equally suspect, and in the end he asked me what I was doing first – although the binoculars and telescope must have given me away.

It turned out that the man was called Roger, and he was a local with a healthily rustic accent; I guessed that he was in his fifties and, judging by his tanned, well-wrinkled face, he was a confirmed man of the outdoors.

It was true. 'I've been catching eels', he said and led me to a truck parked up by The Weir. He lifted a tarpaulin and there, entombed in ice, was a rack full of the snake-like fish. Eyes wide open, they looked up with that gormless, uninterested look that is so typical of fish, even when they are alive. I was surprised at how large the eels were; some were approaching a metre long, and they had an ample girth of silvery flesh. I had not seen an eel since childhood and in my ignorance did not realize that they even occurred along my stretch of The River.

'Have you just caught them on a line?' I asked.

He shook his head. 'No, I've left traps overnight across The Weir. In fact, they've been out for the last four nights. I've caught 200 kilograms of eels.'

I raised my eyebrows dutifully, having not a clue as to

whether this was good or not. 'Do you do this for a living?' I ventured.

'What, catch eels?' he responded, almost laughing. 'If I did only that I wouldn't last long. The season is just a few weeks. The eels are migrating downstream; it'll be over soon.'

Roger had cottoned on by now to the fact that I was an ichthyological ignoramus, and explained more about the life history of the humble eel.

'These eels are heading out to sea to breed,' he said. 'They go to the Sargasso Sea, across the Atlantic. That's where they spawn, and then the eggs hatch and come back in a few years as young eels, or elvers, which eventually go back upstream. Right, I need to get going on my delivery.' With that, he mounted his truck and headed off, presumably to the nearest posh restaurant where the fish would be on the menu by evening.

As Roger drove off, I resolved to find out more about the movements of the eel population of The Patch. I had often thought long and hard about bird migrants, such as woodpigeons, but I had never guessed that, at the same time as birds were heading out to sea, directly below them certain fish were doing the same. The marvels of the sky were being mirrored by the marvels of the water.

The eels that Roger was catching were so-called yellow eels, adult eels that have spent ten years or more in quiet ponds and the upper reaches of Britain's rivers, feeding up and putting on weight. Having matured, they swim downstream to salt water in the autumn, and are thought then to make their way to that strangely isolated backwater of the Atlantic Ocean, not far off the Bahamas, known as the Sargasso Sea. There has been some dispute in the past as to whether these fish are actually capable of the 5,000 kilometre journey, not least because their gut apparently dissolves en route and they don't feed. However, they have recently been satellite-tracked for the first 1,300 kilometres of their route and, cunningly, the eels don't actually head directly to their destination, but instead track south-west to close to the Azores, where it is possible that they hitch a ride on a fast ocean current that whisks them to their spawning grounds.

Whatever the facts of the adults' journey, there is no doubt that, in the Sargasso Sea, hundreds of millions of eel eggs hatch out as larvae. The larvae are completely dissimilar from the adult fish and for a long time they were classified as a completely different organism, a leptocephalus (the larval stage is still called a leptocephalus today). They are tiny, just five millimetres long, part of the plankton and almost entirely transparent; their long body is flattened, roughly into the shape of one of those flying seeds, such as a sycamore. Once hatched, the leptocephali drift to the surface and begin the long haul back to the European continent, being carried along by the Gulf Stream. They feed on planktonic organisms and gradually grow to a length of just over seven centimetres, by which time they have reached the waters of the Continental Shelf. At this point they turn into something vaguely resembling an eel, and actually become shorter and rounder. After losing weight they then feed hungrily and gain it again, and become the well-known elvers. These youngsters find their way back to fresh water and eventually work their way upriver, to the same places that the adult eels vacated in order to travel to the spawning grounds. Indeed, back in the spring, elvers doubtless made their way past the very weir where Roger collected the full-grown eels today.

The round-trip of the common eels is remarkable enough, what with its great distance and the need to adapt to different levels of salinity. In recent years, though, those satellite-tracking experiments have added still more wonder to the mix. When the adult eels leave the fresh water and reach the edge of the Continental Shelf, it seems that they metamorphose to become deep-water fish, acquiring larger eyes. They also acquire longer pectoral fins for swimming efficiency and their skin becomes silvery, to make them harder to see from above. The tracking found that the eels did indeed dive deep, down to about a kilometre below the surface. But this only happened during the day. At night the eels swam up to the 200–300 metre layer, where the water was warmer, before descending into the cold water at dawn. This extraordinary topsy-turvy diurnal shift was a complete surprise. The speculation is that the eels swim in the warm water to keep up their metabolic rate, while swimming in deep, cold water delays their sexual maturation. In other words, they cannot mate and form eggs, which would make them too plump to migrate efficiently to the spawning grounds.

There are still quite a number of mysteries concerning the migration of eels. For a start, nobody has ever actually caught a common eel in the ocean, let alone an individual close to the spawning grounds in the Sargasso Sea. They have only been found in the stomach of the odd sperm whale and deep-sea fish. Furthermore, the swimming speed so far recorded by the satellite-tracked eels has not been fast enough to get the fish to the spawning grounds in time for the early spring spawning – that is why they are thought to hitch a ride on a cross-ocean current. In common with research into other great scientific enigmas, newly acquired information only raises more questions.

So, what with puzzling pigeons and slippery eels, it was a day for wondering, beside an ordinary wood and an ordinary river in an unheralded slip of southern England.

Friday 20 November 2009

Much as I think November is underrated as a birding month, I did not expect this time of year to produce any unexpected visitors. November typically sees high volumes of birds moving about, but normally they consist of standard winter fare, such as finches, or thrushes such as redwings and fieldfares – big crowds, familiar faces.

It was a surprise, therefore, to get a tip-off yesterday about another new species for The Patch, to go with the pipit a couple of weeks ago. It was even more of a surprise that the bird has been patronizing the newly laid out car park for the Visitor Centre, which hardly qualifies as typical birding habitat. Yet again, birds have this capacity to surprise that seems never to run out. It's pure joy.

The fact is, though, that if any bird disabuses expectations of habitat use, it's this particular character, the black redstart. At heart a bird of mountains, cliffs and rocky slopes, it seems to have managed to adapt to man-made 'mountains', namely buildings and concrete constructions in urban areas and industrial sites. Where in uplands it will use rocky prominences from which to perch and seek food, in the lowlands it will translate to something similar, such as piles of boulders or gravel, or even machinery. Somehow the black redstart doesn't just tolerate the broken and littered landscapes of neglected Britain, it may actually be attracted to them.

The black redstart would thus probably be a common species here if it wasn't for its need for a strong supply of insects year-round; we are at the border of its climatic tolerance in Britain. Instead, it is destined always to be a rarity, or at least a notable species, usually just passing through. And the bird seen at The Patch yesterday was undoubtedly a passage migrant, probably one blown over from Holland or Belgium on north-east winds, an individual on its way to the Mediterranean to spend a gentle winter.

Happily for me, a quick look in the car park is enough to relocate this splendid bird, in the company of The Patch's site manager and manic angling enthusiast, Ian. Ian mixes friendly joviality with an unmistakable whiff of irony, and he tries commendably hard to get excited about what is essentially a small, brown, robin-like bird perching on a wire fence just outside his office. To the connoisseur, the black redstart is a small brown bird that sports its very own hue of dark sooty-brown, which almost completely clothes it. However, the tail is orange, and is constantly shivered in a slightly feverish way, which presumably signals one individual's presence to another. The shivering is unique to the black redstart and its close relative, the common redstart, but I have to admit that I'm not having much success in selling this visitor's charms to Ian. He soon retreats back to his office and back, I suspect, to thinking about fish.

It's a curious fact of patch-watching life that the keenest among us often fail to find unusual things. In the case of this black redstart, a man visiting The Lake for almost the first time turned it up, which I find mortifying. It's really the job of the patch-watcher-on-site to find most of the birds, and missing such a good species feels like something of a failure, and undermines my confidence in the sharpness of my own birding ability. I am comforted, though, in realizing that visiting-birder-finding-rarity syndrome seems to happen all the time, to enthusiasts everywhere. The only suitable explanation that I have ever heard is that regular patch-watchers get so caught up in the normal ebb and flow of what they see and expect to see that, when the abnormal happens, they manage to overlook it.

Or they could be plain unlucky. The only truly rare bird (in national terms) that has ever turned up at my Patch is a great egret, which looks, as you might expect, like a giant version of a little egret and flies with imperiously slow wing-beats. One was reported in *Bird Watching* magazine from 11 November 2006, but I never got details of the record or who sent it in. It was presumably near The Lake because, on that very same day, I decided to check out The Quarry, and I missed it. The species is becoming commoner in Britain and there will be chances for it to turn up at The Patch again, I'm sure – but the miss hurts badly, even so.

DECEMBER

Tuesday 1 December 2009

A wildlife-watcher could make the case for any month of the year being special, except possibly this one. Yes, the signs of spring do increase day by day, and the shortest day heralds the hidden start to spring, but it is also dark and damp and a little depressing. Frankly, December is most enjoyable when its end is in sight. It seems a little hard to appreciate a month only for what it offers in the future, but for us it is a reality, and it probably is for the birds, too.

Thank goodness for robins. They are astonishingly prominent at this time of year. They are on the front of our cards, and out in the wild they are perhaps thriving in the damp soil. They visit bird-tables and fluff out their feathers, and it seems that we really cannot miss them. The other day our family spotted a robin at the nearby garden centre; we were buying a Christmas tree at the time.

Out on The Patch, the robin is one of the few birds singing. Admittedly, towards the end of the month there will be some other species joining in the chorus, but the robin is now quite dominant, especially at dusk, and on still afternoons. The robin is the bird that people often hear singing at night in their gardens and wrongly assume to be a nightingale (a summer migrant currently in Africa). The two species are closely related; they both have large eyes and are used to foraging in low light levels. While vocally the robin is a poor-man's nightingale, at least it is here now, singing – a spirited vocalist for the dark days and their twilight.

The scientists have found that male robins sometimes change their tune and their singing post in December and start to attract a mate, instead of simply being endlessly territorial and bad tempered. If a female responds the male will at first tolerate her presence, and then there will be some display. It's called song-and-following; the male sings and then hops to a different perch, the female chases him. Once this happens, and especially once the incumbent male tolerates the female by his side, the pair can be assumed officially to have formed.

There won't be any proper breeding behaviour yet. Indeed, the female will return to her own territory for much of the time, and the earliest the newly formed pair might meet up again with intent is in March. Yet, what passes between them is an official pairing; you might quite rightly call it an engagement. The two parties will not look for another mate: their union is sealed.

However, like everything this month, they are looking to the future.

Tuesday 15 December 2009

I tried to go birding today, but the cold was perishing and it's December. As you may know, birding takes more effort in December than any other month, because birders tend to get enthusiastic about New Years, not old ones. It's like working for a boss whom you know is about to retire; you're treading water.

I retreated into the Visitor Centre to get warm, chatting to Ian, who sat cradling his cup of tea and nursing the mother of all colds. There are very few days in the year when I don't envy Ian for living and working here at The Patch, but today, at least, is one of them.

I wandered around the conference room and my eye caught a display case in the corner. As I leaned over it, an artefact reflected the history of the local area, and I began to think hard about yesteryear. And most especially, having such an interest in natural things, I wondered what sort of animals and birds must have once lived upon this spot? Only fifteen years ago, this place was a field by a river. A hundred years ago it was an isolated patch of countryside. There are Bronze Age (roughly 3,000-year-old) burial grounds on The Patch. What was the countryside like then? Probably farmed, open country, with lots of sheep and goats. In Mesolithic times it was probably part of the wildwood, and going back further, what mighty creatures could have passed this way, during the Ice Ages and even before?

Everywhere in Britain has a long story to tell like this, and The Patch is no different. Happily for us, records of animal life in Britain are reasonably accurate compared to many parts of the world. For instance, we know (or at least suspect) that rabbits did not reach Britain until 1066, when they came in with the Normans. What a change! Rabbits are superabundant at The Patch, and it would be easy to think they have been here forever.

There were some pretty remarkable animals around during the Bronze Age, and there's no doubt that they would have occurred nearby, even if they didn't actually set foot upon what is now The Patch. Many of them are extinct, but a few, such as roe deer and lots of the small mammals, would have been here for most or all of this time. Imagine the case of the wood mouse, for example. This small creature could easily have been on the very same ground continuously since perhaps 10,000 years ago, or even more. That gives us some perspective on who actually owns the land!

The Bronze Age people would have had some interesting neighbours. One of these, the aurochs, was a type of wild cattle with very large, handlebar horns, which lived in the woodland. It used to occur over much of central Europe, including Britain, but became extinct around 1627. Bones have been found fairly close by, and it sends shivers down the spine to think that a species of large mammal could have trodden over the same bedrock that underlies The Patch today, but has since been wiped off the face of the earth by human activity, mainly hunting. It puts current conservation projects into sharp relief.

Another animal to keep the Bronze Age inhabitants on their toes – or at least, their livestock on their toes – was the lynx, the last magnificent big cat still to survive in Europe, although now long extinct in Britain. There were also wolves and bears about, which again must have stalked the settlers' animals and engendered great fear among the human population. Wolves were still around in England up until about the fourteenth century, and they are such wide-ranging animals that they would certainly have occurred on The Patch.

The truth is that an argument could be made for all sorts of wild animals having stomped around any tiny part of Britain. It is intellectually exhilarating to analyse what once was but, even more so, it is a thrill to visit the corners of our imagination and come face to face with awesome creatures, knowing that it is only time, not length, breadth or height, that has come between us and the real thing. Large mammals really did tread here, where you and I might cast our feet lightly and ponder silly, minor irritations in this world.

But how much more of a frisson would you feel if you knew for sure – with absolute certainty – that your patch had indeed hosted the mighty? And that is why a look at the cabinet in the conference room had thrown me into such a state of historical contemplation. For during the excavation of the gravel pit, the workers had found the real tusk of none other than a woolly mammoth. This impressive beast was either here, or its body was washed here. The tusk had lain in anonymous gravel deposits for at least 10,000 years, since a time when The Patch was so completely a different place that it might have been on a different planet.

But it wasn't on a different planet. It was right here, and only the passage of years makes it seem distant.

Wednesday 30 December 2009

The year is fading away, and with the enchantment of January just around the corner, it is tempting to ignore The Patch until the day after tomorrow, when all the birds will once again be New for the Year. After nearly a hundred visits, can this small area really provide anything of interest at the very end of a period of intensive watching?

Gloriously, it can. As I was wandering absent-mindedly along The River in the fading afternoon light, copying the waterway's meanders, I spotted a movement in thick vegetation just above the water-level, and realized straight away that I was eye to eye with a Cetti's warbler, undoubtedly The Patch's most elusive bird species. Despite having heard its distinctive song many times – it shouts out a short, melodious phrase to the rhythm of the first few bars of *Eine Kleine Nachtmusik* – I had never set eyes on one on The Patch before, and was delightfully taken aback.

Nobody would choose a Cetti's warbler from a bird book and pick it out as the species they would most like to see above all others. It is, after all, small and brown. And despite a big tail, and even a touch of grey on the side of the head, it doesn't look any different from an awful lot of other birds. But it is famously skulking, to such an extent that I know some birdwatchers who have seen as many Cetti's as they have yetis, which is precisely none. The Cetti's warbler's most celebrated trick is to sing very loudly from thick vegetation close by a group of birdwatchers, and then fall teasingly silent as its potential admirers search every stem and leaf for movement, becoming increasingly infuriated. Then, just as the humans are about to give up, the bird shouts out again from a different bush a few metres away, again tantalizingly close. Encouraged, the victims repeat the searching process, wondering how they can possibly have failed to see the singer. After the last pair of binoculars goes down, the bird sings yet again, and so on until both sets of participants get fed up with the game, one of them disappearing smugly off to feed, and the others disappearing disconsolately off to do the same, in a cafe. There are birdwatchers who swear that the Cetti's warbler is a conspiracy created by loudspeakers.

But the conspiracy was alive and perky today. It hopped around at the base of some rushes, almost stepping on to an adjacent floating mat of vegetative die-off, foraging for its usual diet of small waterside invertebrates. Its large, dark eyes and its habit of constantly cocking up its ample tail gave it a distinctly wren-like appearance, albeit a wren that has been pumping steroids. Quite what had induced it to blow its usual paranoid cover and allow the faint daylight to shine upon it for a few moments I have no idea. Perhaps it, too, had succumbed to the universal end-of-year apathy?

The Cetti's warbler is one of those species that explodes the myth that small brown birds live colourless lives. Its life history is unusual in a number of respects, not least that, while almost every other warbler in the region timidly evacuates Britain for warmer climes during the winter, the Cetti's warbler sits out the cold months, eking a living within the tangled labyrinths of waterside vegetation, as it is doing today. The Cetti's is, therefore, a tough operator. It also has a complicated private life, eschewing the simplicity of monogamy for a breeding system of meritocracy which is almost capitalist in its ruthlessness. Males are up to 20 per cent heavier than females (one of the biggest differences found in any small bird in the world), and the number of mates that they attract and inseminate is largely dependent on their own body weight, and presumably their quality. In one study, about 20 per cent of males in a population managed to acquire a single mate in a given year, 30 per cent acquired two, a further 20 per cent acquired three mates or more, and a few bloated individuals did even better than that. Of course, that leaves at least 25 per cent that failed to attract a mate at all, small brown birds abandoned on the shelf – which is a bit hard considering that they had the success of surviving a British winter on their CV. But that is the cruelty of mate choice for you.

There are, so far as I know, only two male Cetti's warblers on The Patch, so perhaps there is less dog-eat-dog competition in this recently settled parcel of habitat? Who knows? The fact is, these birds are so secretive that I have no idea how many females could be living along our kilometre or so stretch of riverside. Maybe both males have four willing partners each? It's one of the many undercover stories that are locked away in every small parcel of hinterland.

I left the Cetti's warbler to the waterside tangles, wishing it the best for the breeding season to come. The light faded and The River seemed to slow down to a state of sluggish torpor. The world, it seems, is waiting for the year to end.

Thursday 31 December 2009

I have come out to put the year to bed – just a quick walk around half The Lake, to watch the natural world wind down. A curious thing is the dusk of New Year's Eve. It's a special dusk only in our minds; the newness of tomorrow is manufactured, but it feels no less special for it.

This evening witnesses the typical comings and goings of every mid-winter dusk, when the diurnal creatures swap with the nocturnal ones. (Tonight, though, one diurnal animal, man,

183

becomes unusually nocturnal, for one night only). I am fortunate to catch a glimpse of one of the nocturnal shift-workers, a fox, which scuttles away across The Shire Field in a preoccupied manner. This is an animal that might just see the New Year in with a night of special personal significance. Now is the height of its breeding season, and the nights of late December and January offer a surprisingly narrow window of just a few weeks for mating. The vixens are fertile for this very short part of the year, and so genuine opportunities for a successful insemination for mating foxes are precious.

The fox is a lucky sighting, because on most dusk visits the scene is dominated by birds on their way to roost. And while the daytime is undoubtedly winding down, the scene is more feverish than sleepy; there is urgency, not slackening, in the cold, damp air. There could be an analogy with the human working world and the mad evening rush-hour; while everybody commuting is relieved that work is over and is looking forward to getting home, it is far from an easing down. It is bad-tempered and almost desperate. In the same way, the journey to the roost site, and the so-called settling down, can be one of the most stressful parts of the day for a bird.

Think of the blackbirds in your garden. As the light fades these birds begin to make loud 'chinking' calls, which are the same calls they make when they find a cat or an owl during the daytime. You might think that the noisy 'chinks' are calls of fear or warning, but they are actually angry, and when they echo from the depths of trees or bushes at dusk, they betray the mood within the blackbird roost. Blackbirds usually sleep in small groups, each bird separated from the next by a few tens of centimetres, but they aren't amicable gatherings. Instead the birds argue and fight over the best and safest perches for sleeping, competing hard for the most favourable microclimate. The atmosphere as the birds settle is tense and cruel.

The same sort of thing happens in gatherings of rooks. Again, there is much competition over the very best places to sleep. It turns out that the dominant birds always get the best places, while the subordinates suffer and seethe. On a cold, windy night, dominant rooks park themselves in the middle of a tree, while the subordinates have to make do with the chilly outer branches. On a windless night, however, the roles are reversed. The dominant rooks perch on the outer branches of the tree, while the subordinates are forced to take the perches below them. During the night the rooks digest their pre-roost meal, and the waste products are excreted *in situ*. The dominant rooks literally poo upon the subordinates below.

Roosting politics even occur in what would seem to be the most amicable possible of all bird flocks, long-tailed tits. In contrast to other species, these mites live in family flocks during the winter, rather than forming aggregations of unrelated strangers, which is the norm for just about every other bird species. The groups consist of the breeding pair and their progeny from the previous breeding season, plus a few brothers or sisters of the adult male. At night these exceptionally small-bodied birds actually huddle together in bodily contact to pool and save energy, something that is highly unusual among birds, which usually keep apart. The long-tailed tits can all be seen to sit in a line, tails pointing down the same way, feathers fluffed out as if the whole family were sharing a duvet. Yet even here there is a hierarchy, for the centre of a huddle is a much warmer place than the edge of a huddle, and the mid-huddle bird will have a better chance of surviving a cold night than a bird on the edge. And while you might expect parent birds to want to place their precious children into the safe centre of the huddle, it doesn't work like that. The dominant parents hog the centre, and the rest take their chances, squabbling over the peripheral spots.

Roosting battles can be intensely personal. You might well have read that wrens, among the smallest of all British birds, will also huddle together for warmth on the coldest, longest winter nights, and famously, up to fifty or sixty can occasionally be found sharing the confined space of a nest-box. In fact the wren is a hot-blooded character, and will only do this when its survival depends on a huddle. Any wren would rather not huddle at all and, remarkably, it seems that wrens actually draw the line at huddling with certain individuals. Studies have shown that, when a wren accepts that it needs to share its roost site with others, it will stand nearby the entrance and act like a doorman, monitoring the numbers and different individuals that enter. Some potential entrants are, it seems, refused permission by the owner to come in. For some reason, their face either doesn't fit, or maybe they have visible health problems, or perhaps there is history between individuals. Either way, it could potentially be very serious for the bird refused entry.

These examples give an indication of just how important the dusk is for birds, and explains the level of activity. A good many species also partake of a major evening meal, packing in as much feeding as they can before the light fades; starlings, for example, do this in large flocks on grassland. Many birds also try to have a bath. It might look like madness to soak the feathers in the rapidly dropping temperatures, but birds are well insulated and recent experiments have shown that a bath actually keeps the feathers in tip-top condition, and allows the wearers to be more efficient at escaping from predators should they be attacked. It all goes to show how crucial the evening routine is for birds.

While it can be difficult to see small, secretive birds such as wrens and blue tits going to their roost sites, the comings and goings of others are very obvious. The rush-hour over The Patch consists of a number of different species making commuting movements. There will be flights of crows, rooks and jackdaws, starlings and gulls, even pied wagtails and green-finches making their way over The Lake to different locations: the starlings to bushes, the rooks to trees and the gulls to the sea. There is nothing special about The Lake in this context. In patches throughout the country, over the last half hour to hour of light, the same thing happens. It is one of the great wildlife movements of Britain, barely appreciated and scarcely witnessed. It's not quite as spectacular as a wildebeest migration, admittedly, but its scale is simply enormous.

Here at The Lake, where the land is slightly elevated and it is easy to look over the darkening fields to the west, with suburbia in other directions, the bearings that different birds take can be obvious. Their destinations, though, can be a mystery. For example, every night at least twenty or thirty pied wagtails fly over The Lake heading in a westerly direction, but I have no idea where they go. Perhaps they are heading for the underpass of a major road a little further away, or perhaps they are heading for the flat roof of a garage or supermarket? At this time of year pied wagtails have the endearing habit of roosting in Christmas trees, utilizing the small but significant heat output of the coloured lights. There is no shortage of these around at the moment.

There is something reassuring to a birdwatcher about watching the evening traffic. If fifty rooks pass over in their usual way, in a short stream, the sort of movement that would occur when a business seminar broke up and everybody went to lunch, forming short-lived associations linked by snatches of conversation, then everything is well with rooks. If the gulls take off from The Lake and assume pleasing formations against the setting sun, as they fly-cum-amble down towards the coast, then I know all is well with the gulls. The finches lollop down to the bushes astride The Quarry, where they disappear into The Thicket and are safe for the night. In the darkness the Canada geese take off from fields far away and make their way to the waters of The Lake, making their unmusical honks and reminding me irresistibly of a party of noisy drunks spewing out from a nightclub. They land with a splash and excite a few irritable calls from the perpetually angry coots – and I know that if the coots are angry then they are safe, too. All is well with the world.

Then there are the starlings. The Patch doesn't witness large movements of starlings, not the theatrical swirls that occur at large roosts and find their way without fail on to the autumn TV screens. There must be large roosts nearby, but I am not sure of their location. Instead, all we get is a stream of small parties of starlings heading away to the west, their very unhesitant flight suggesting that they still have some way to go to reach their colleagues. What is certain is that they will go to meet hordes of their own kind, form bird swarms and paint abstract patterns in the sky somewhere.

The great assemblies of starlings are yet another example of a great wildlife phenomenon that can be witnessed in this country – a well-known spectacle the true function of which, like so many, is still something of a mystery. We really don't know why starlings roost together instead of finding a cosy personal hole in a tree and settling down there. There has to be a good reason. Knowing how important a roost site is to a bird – a matter of life and death, no less – there has to be a glaring reason to gather in conspicuous multitudes and spend the hours of darkness with birds that are rivals and carriers of potential disease. True, being in a large flock does make an individual statistically less likely to be taken by a predator than if it is alone or in a small flock, but at the same time large gatherings statistically attract more predators than are likely to come upon a lone bird. Except on the coldest evenings, starlings probably don't make use of huddling with their colleagues, and they are not known to benefit from any microclimate formed by an aggregation of large birds.

Why do they do it, then? The best theory at present is that the roost site acts as some kind of information exchange. Perhaps the birds don't talk to each other, but there is every chance that birds in a roost, tightly packed and in the faces of many others, can monitor each other's fitness and condition. The idea goes that, should a starling meet an unusually healthy and well-fed bird in the roost, it could then choose to follow that colleague to its feeding sites in the morning, and benefit from its new acquaintance's knowledge of well-stocked foraging areas. It's a good theory, but tricky to prove and hard to square with the idea of hierarchies and those closely knit units of starlings that come to feed on our lawns. Wouldn't a healthy bird want to keep its feeding grounds a secret, and wouldn't an unwieldy mass of birds follow the healthiest individuals each day, leading to disproportionately sized feeding groups and anarchy among hungry hangers-on? Somehow, it doesn't seem quite to fit reality.

I have said many times that one of the delights of patch-watching is how everyday observations of wildlife can lead quickly to questions and ultimately to mysteries. The starlings are a good example. They aren't particularly common birds on my Patch, and as mentioned earlier, they don't perform the aerial histrionics over this parcel of ground that elsewhere makes them so famous. But they pass by and, as such, they are still Patch species, and Patch individuals. Just as swallows migrate from The Patch on a great journey, a journey that is part of the natural history of this land by dint of their appearance here as migrants, so the starlings' astonishing behaviour elsewhere is still part of the natural history fabric of The Patch itself.

The thing is, my own Patch isn't confined to its physical limitations of time and space. The many birds and animals that pass by ensure that it is really much bigger than that. No wildlife-watcher, however confined, is ever bound by limitations such as borders and boundaries. The watchers can go with the wildlife, in their imagination, to the ends of the earth and to the borders of scientific knowledge.

Darkness envelops The Patch as some tardy carrion crows flap silently westward, the last of the day-shift. All the daylight of the year has gone, and now only the lights of the houses and streets twinkle on the water surface of The Lake. In twelve hours all the commuting will start again. The reassuring cycle of day and year rolls on.

INDEX